HOME
REPAIRS AND
IMPROVEMENTS

HOME
REPAIRS AND
IMPROVEMENTS

Edited by R. H. Allen

MARSHALL CAVENDISH

Please note:

We have taken great care to ensure that the information in this book is accurate. However, since building regulations, local bye-laws and the construction of individual houses vary so greatly, we can accept no responsibility for loss or damage caused by the misapplication of any instruction.

This edition published in 1993
by Marshall Cavendish Books
(A division of Marshall Cavendish
Partworks Ltd)
119 Wardour Street
London W1V 3TD

ISBN 1 85435 389 6

Printed and Bound in Malaysia

CONTENTS

INTRODUCTION

Home improvement has two main results: to improve the quality of life in your home; and to increase the value of the property. Carrying out these improvements yourself has the additional result of giving you the satisfaction of enjoying your own workmanship for years to come. This book sets out to give you full instructions for completing a variety of projects with confidence.

The book is arranged in sections, each containing a selection of 'new' projects and maintenance tasks. Take a kitchen, for example—the first room in many a house to receive attention. In the Home Plumber section you will find instructions for curing a dripping tap and plumbing in a washing machine. Would the room be more convenient if the door opened the other way? The Home Carpenter section tells you how to rehang a door and make any necessary repairs to it. Condensation and cooking smells can be a problem—you will find instructions for installing an extractor fan in Home Builder. And what use would an extractor fan be without electricity? Home Electrician solves that problem and gives details of the wiring circuits for a selection of kitchen appliances. There is also a comprehensive index for locating information that may not necessarily have a full article devoted to it.

Before attempting any of the projects, it is a good idea to read through the instructions from start to finish to give yourself a clear idea of what is involved. If, after doing so, you are unsure of your capabilities, try to enlist the help of a friend with more experience of such things— you can learn so much in this way and boost your confidence to tackle a similar job yourself the next time. This is especially important in the case of electricity where mistakes can have serious consequences—if in doubt, contact a qualified electrician!

If you are a novice at DIY, tackle the simple jobs first before attempting the more ambitious ones and enjoy your achievements. If you are an old hand, you will find this book an invaluable source of reference. Whatever the level of your skill, you will find here ways to improve and maintain the value of any home. Applying a little time and money now can bring great benefits in the years to come.

PLANNING A SHOWER

● Where to site a shower ● Problems of water supply ● Coping with temperature fluctuations ● Problems of drainage ● Installing a shower base and instantaneous shower

Taking a shower is the ideal way to freshen up, much more convenient than having a bath and considerably cheaper. Among the other benefits of a shower are its constant running temperature, and the possibility of fitting it away from the bathroom to avoid early-morning congestion.

You have the choice of converting existing room space to form an enclosure (fig. A), or of buying one of the many prefabricated enclosures (fig. B) now on the market—many of which come complete with fixtures and fittings.

If you plan to make your own enclosure, base the design of this on the use of a prefabricated shower base. This considerably simplifies the all-important drainage arrangements, which are often the greatest problem where the bath is not used. From a

safety point of view, make sure you provide adequate lighting and room for movement.

On the plumbing side, hot and cold water supply pipes have to be laid on as well as drainage, and these points go a long way towards influencing your choice of site. At the shower, the hot and cold water can be mixed by

> **WARNING: AUSTRALIA & NEW ZEALAND**
> Electrical, plumbing and drainage work is required by Australian & NZ building regulations and supply authority rules to be carried out only by a licensed tradesperson. It should be stressed that unlicensed tradespersons must not undertake the work outlined here.

A. *Purpose-built shower enclosure, here incorporating an 'instant' electric heater*

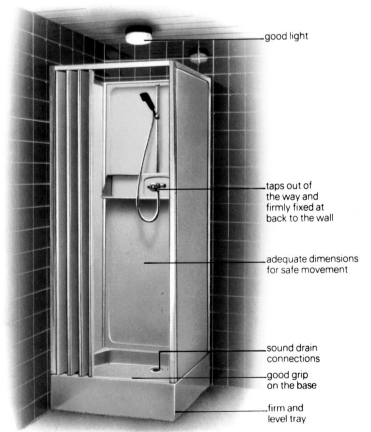

good light

taps out of the way and firmly fixed at back to the wall

adequate dimensions for safe movement

sound drain connections

good grip on the base

firm and level tray

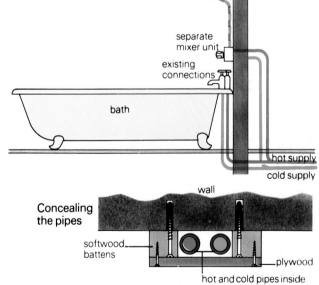

separate mixer unit

existing connections

bath

hot supply

cold supply

wall

Concealing the pipes

softwood battens

plywood

hot and cold pipes inside

B. Left: *A prefabricated shower base can be located wherever plumbing and drainage present no problem. Observe commonsense safety precautions*
C. *If you choose to use your bath as a shower base, an independent hot and cold water supply permits some freedom in locating this. Box off exposed piping as shown*

D. *Interrupting existing hot and cold water supplies in order to feed the shower control requires some care. Mixer controls should be fed by independent hot and cold water supplies wherever possible to avoid water starvation—hence temperature fluctuations—when taps in other parts of the system are turned on. To ensure equal hot and cold water tap pressures at the mixer, see that the cold water supply comes from the same system as supplies the hot water system, or from one alongside it. The two diagrams show two typical supply interruption points. Adequate water pressure is essential: the head of water must be at least a metre, but preferably more for optimum flow. Raising the supply cistern is one way of achieving this*

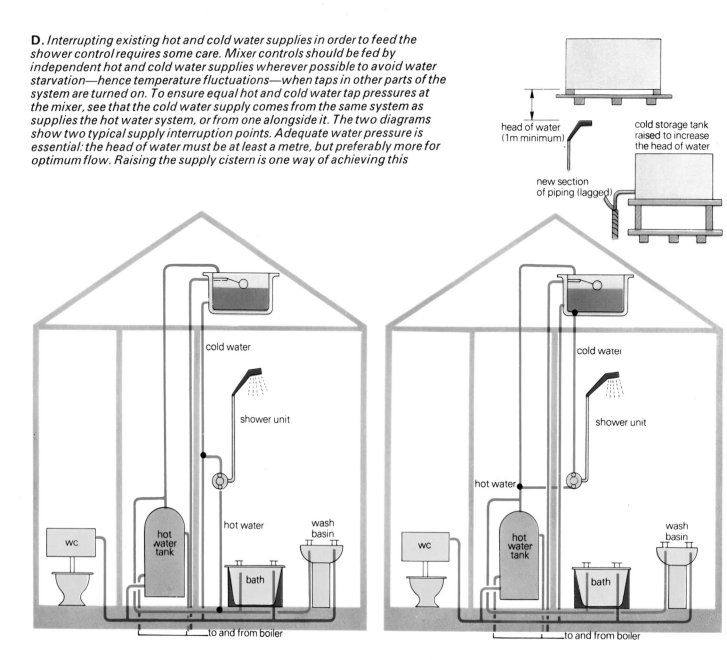

head of water (1m minimum)

new section of piping (lagged)

cold storage tank raised to increase the head of water

cold water

shower unit

hot water

wash basin

WC

hot water tank

bath

to and from boiler

cold water

shower unit

hot water

wash basin

WC

hot water tank

bath

to and from boiler

independent taps or by a single control. Supply pipework and the shower head connection can be concealed beneath tiling, perhaps behind a false panel fixed to the wall.

Another alternative is to provide a shower over a bath, either by fitting combination bath/shower mixer taps in place of the existing taps, or by laying on piping for an independent shower. With this arrangement, you have no shower base or drainage to worry about.

If it is difficult or impossible to lay on a suitable hot water supply, then an electric 'instantaneous' shower or gas heater may provide the answer, although both have disadvantages compared to a two-pipe shower. The

instantaneous electric shower has a slower flow rate, and the gas shower needs ducting to the outside (it is usually attached to an outer wall). However, instantaneous showers have improved dramatically over the past few years and are well worth considering.

The water supply
For proper operation of a shower, there must be sufficient water pressure at the shower rose. In many British houses, the water pressure at most taps (both hot and cold) is provided by a cold water storage cistern, mounted above the level of the water outlets. The higher the cistern above the outlet, the greater the pressure will be; the vertical distance measured from the

bottom of the cistern to the outlet is called the *head*. For a shower, the head is measured to the rose and ideally should not be less than 1.5m, though in simple plumbing systems a head of 1m may be sufficient.

If the head is between about 1m and 1.5m, then an adequate shower may be achieved if you can keep connecting pipework runs short, and with very few bends.

For heads of less than a metre, or where it is not possible to have short simple pipe runs, there are three main solutions. The first is to install a *flow booster*—a type of electrical pump which increases the pressure. Operation is automatic.

The second solution is to *increase the*

height of the cold water storage cistern by raising it up on a sturdy wooden platform. But there may not be room in your loft to do this. Another solution is to use an *instantaneous shower* connected directly to the cold water mains.

In some areas of the UK, houses do not have cold water storage cisterns; instead, all cold taps and so on are supplied direct from the mains. Hot taps are usually supplied from a conventional hot water cylinder fed from its own small cistern. Direct water systems such as these will have different requirements. For example, with this arrangement it is not possible to fit a conventional mixer type shower: it would contravene water regulations. You can either fit an instantaneous shower or perhaps modify your plumbing so that the shower is fed from a suitable, conventional cold water storage cistern.

In Australia, the whole system, including the hot supply, is fed direct from the mains, and showers designed to work with this system are readily available. In Britain, a fully direct system like this will almost certainly use a 'multipoint' type gas heater: you should consult both your gas board and your water authority about the possible problems of connecting a shower to such a supply.

Temperature fluctuations
Water starvation in either hot or cold supply pipes can cause temperature fluctuations in the shower, which could be annoying or even dangerous. It is very sensible to buy a shower that is thermostatically controlled, or at least has a temperature limiting device so that the water never gets dangerously hot.

For showers in an indirect plumbing system, it is a good idea to use separate hot and cold supply pipes that do not feed any other fittings—then turning on any other taps in the home will have no effect on the flow.

Drainage considerations
Although deciding how to supply water to a shower can be tricky, it is usually possible to get over the problems one way or another. Leading the dirty water away, though, to a soil stack or waste water drain often presents far more constraints. PVC piping, being easy to work with, is the logical choice for this sort of job. But breaking through walling, both internal and external, is usually necessary if the discharge pipe is to remain completely

E. *A built-in shower enclosure is a desirable feature of any well-appointed bathroom, but can of course be incorporated wherever there is room to spare. Note the hinged screen of strengthened or laminated glass*

hidden from view. And unlike hot and cold supply piping, the discharge branch cannot be taken under the floorboards unless the run is between, and almost parallel to, the joists underneath.

Your choice of site for the shower must therefore take into consideration drainage arrangements almost to the exclusion of everything else.

In Britain, the Building Regulations limit the run of the branch discharge pipe to a length of 3 metres and to a slope of between 1° and 5° (equivalent to a drop of between 18mm and 90mm per metre length).

An 'S' trap can be employed if a pipe drop is required (fig. G), such as when underfloor drainage is possible, but otherwise a 'P' trap is preferable—shallow ones are available if space is tight. Use pipe of 42mm diameter.

If the shower base discharge pipe can be arranged to go directly through the wall and connection has to be made to an outside soil stack or waste hopper, much of the fall can be arranged externally.

Use professional help if you have

to break into a cast-iron stack, though it is usually easier to replace the whole stack with the PVC equivalent so that the shower and any future additions to the system involve the minimum amount of work.

Installing a shower base
The first stage of the job is to prepare structural work—such as a timber frame for the enclosure—if this is necessary. Thereafter the sequence is:

In the UK, alterations to existing plumbing installations are strictly controlled by local water authority by-laws. Because of this, you should inform your local water board of your plans at least seven days before work starts. As well as giving practical advice, they will warn you against any possible infringement of their regulations.

In addition to this, new waste pipe installations should have Building Regulations approval, which should be obtained from the local authority.

Run hot and cold water supply pipes to the point where a connection is made with the shower controller.

Follow carefully any recommendations made by the shower manufacturer as to where to break in to the supply. Use 15mm copper piping and 'T' connections to connect with your existing hot and cold water pipes, keeping bends to a minimum and pipe runs as short as possible. Use either compression or capillary fittings; they are equally suitable, but you will find that the latter are cheaper, and are certainly neater looking.

Remove the shower base (or tray) and its accessories from the protective wrapping, taking care not to scratch or damage these parts. Lay fixing accessories on the floor close at hand —but not in the immediate working area—in a logical order ready for use.

Lay the shower base on a protective groundsheet, and locate the tubular legs in the sockets welded on each side of the steel shower support frame. Fix the frame to the wooden shower support, which may be flooring grade chipboard (particleboard) or similar.

Secure each leg to its socket upstand using self-tapping screws.

Assemble the adjustable feet but hand tighten only as later adjustment is necessary. Place the base on its feet.

Fix the waste outlet to the shower base, incorporating the sealing washers provided and using a waterproof mastic to complete the seal. Use a holding spanner while tightening the larger nut with an adjustable spanner.

Attach a short length of pipe to the trap and temporarily secure the trap to the waste outlet, then mark on the wall the exit position of the pipe.

Cut a hole through the wall for the discharge pipe at this point (you may wish to enlist professional help here). You will find it easier to remove a small area of skirting first if it is in the way.

Reposition the shower base, then using a bradawl, mark the floor fixing points of its supporting board.

Check the level of the shower base, ensuring that the trap has sufficient ground clearance, and tighten the fixing nut on each leg.

On solid floors it is difficult to drill and plug for eight screws and still have perfect alignment—especially as the holes have to be angled so that the shower base does not impede the actual screwing process. It is easier to fix the support board on its own to the floor, attaching the feet later.

Temporarily link together the trap with a short length of pipe, arranged to protrude through the wall near to where it is to discharge into a hopper or stack. If you have the choice, it's easier to direct the pipe to a hopper.

If discharge is made to a soil stack, mark a point on the stack which is level with the protruding pipe ('A' in fig. G) and another point a little below this so that a drop of between 18 and 90mm per metre is obtained ('B') for satisfactory discharge.

Assemble a replacement triple socket, boss branch and pipe socket and then gauge the length of the piping which has to be removed from the stack in order to fit these. Transfer the measurement to the stack in such a way as to embrace points 'A' and 'B' (fig. G), with the pipe socket coinciding with the latter.

Cut out the stack length with a fine-toothed saw, taking precautions or using assistance to keep the upper and lower lengths in position afterwards.

Dismantle the triple socket from the boss branch and pipe socket. Push the triple socket into the top part of the stack as far as it will go. Then fix the boss branch and pipe branch on to the lower part of the stack. Complete

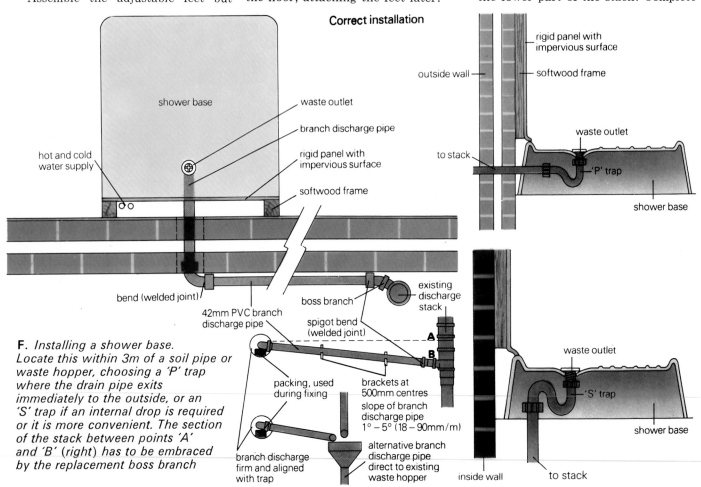

Correct installation

F. *Installing a shower base.
Locate this within 3m of a soil pipe or waste hopper, choosing a 'P' trap where the drain pipe exits immediately to the outside, or an 'S' trap if an internal drop is required or it is more convenient. The section of the stack between points 'A' and 'B' (right) has to be embraced by the replacement boss branch*

G. *A shower enclosure can be incorporated in an under-stairs conversion where other simple washing facilities may also be provided for use by occasional guests. Lack of privacy may pose a problem, however*

the fitting by pushing the triple socket down into its final position.

Insert the spigot bend into the boss branch, attach brackets to the outside connecting length of the discharge pipe and fit this into the spigot bend. Twist the boss branch until the supporting brackets on the discharge pipe make contact with the wall.

The discharge pipe from the inside of the house should by now meet the discharge pipe attached to the stack, and the two can be marked for cutting so that you can fit a 90° bend where the inner pipe leaves the wall. Remove both pipes and cut these to final length.

Replace all pipes, the longer (outside) one with its fixing brackets in place. The shorter (inner) length is fixed first to the trap and then to the bend. Screw the trap to the waste outlet of the shower base. It is essential that all pipes and fittings are perfectly aligned and that no force is used to keep them in place. Make minor adjustments if necessary.

Mark and fix supporting brackets, normally required only for the outside length. Make alignment marks at each of the fittings.

Dismantle pipework and fittings that require solvent welded joints, prepare the joints and reassemble as before.

If the discharge pipe is to be led to an outside hopper, cut the protruding pipe close to the wall and fit a 90° bend. Attach whatever length of pipe is necessary to complete the run to a convenient point above the hopper, and provide support brackets.

Make good the hole through the wall using a proprietary filler paste. There are now aerosol foam sprays on the market which are waterproof, allow for expansion or contraction, and are easier to work with than the more traditional compounds.

Test the pipework, first for stability (proper support and correct joining) and then for watertightness, using a pail of water until connection is made with the supply system.

Connection of the hot and cold water supply pipes to the shower controller (or regulator) is made in the course of assembling the shower enclosure, and the procedures should follow exactly those stipulated by the manufacturer. The valve and spray piping are attached to a mounting panel attached to the wall or set into the wall along with piping. With self-contained shower enclosures, the mounting panel is attached to the rear of the cubicle with a waterproof gasket arrangement.

Completing the enclosure

Once the shower base installation is complete, you can attend to the completion of the shower enclosure. This is a relatively simple job if you are using a prefabricated kit, which often requires little more than a few minutes with a screwdriver. Built-in enclosures requiring woodwork, tiling and other jobs (not forgetting suitable sealing at the joints) take much longer to make but can be matched completely to the design of the room.

Install an electric shower

An instant electric shower is an attractive proposition if use cannot be made of conventional hot and cold water supplies. In most instances, connection of the heater is direct to the mains water supply—so a shower of this type is especially useful if a hot water cylinder is not incorporated within the system. Pressure and flow variations within the system may have a marked effect on temperature stability, however. The heater needs direct and permanent connection to the electricity supply through a double-pole linked switch. The appliance must be earthed, and protected by a 30amp fuse. For additional safety, site the heater well away from the direct spray at the shower, and locate the switch outside the bathroom or shower enclosure.

You can interrupt the rising main at any convenient point. Remember to keep the pipe run as short and as straight as possible. This Deltaflow unit requires a cold water supply which has a minimum static pressure of one bar (equivalent to a water head of about eight metres) which should be available from most mains supplies. In most houses, though, you cannot use a cistern-fed supply because the head will not be great enough.

In Australia and New Zealand you must have electric and plumbing work done by licenced tradesmen. Heater suppliers usually provide a complete installation service.

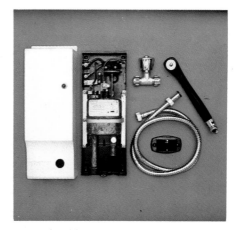

1 *An instant electric shower heater usually comes as a kit of parts. Installation involves plumbing and electrical skills*

2 *Remove the cover and mark the position of the fixing holes, and drill for fixings as required. Knock through for connecting wires*

3 *Cable entry to heater is best made through the rear. Ensure this is correctly wired, tightening the cable clamp securely afterwards*

4 *The double-pole linked switch is located safely on the other side of the wall and connected to the heater via the wall aperture*

5 *Pipe connections near to the heater can be tailor-made to fit. Use capillary fittings up to the point the heater fitting is used*

6 *Interrupt the cold water supply wherever is most convenient, using a 'T' connector. In a loft, lag the pipe well*

7 *Mark the shower rail position and screw the rail firmly into position, with the top of the rail no higher than the heater*

8 *Connect the flexible hose to the water outlet of the heater, turn on the water mains and the flow tap and then check pipework for leaks*

9 *Repeat the procedure with the heater on. Where water pressure is too high, the restrictor may need adjusting to reduce the maximum flow*

10 *When tests have been completed to your satisfaction, finally replace the cover and connect the two neon spade leads*

PLUMBING IN A WASHING MACHINE

● **Choosing the best site** ● **Breaking into the existing water supply** ● **Connecting the hot and cold supplies** ● **Installing the branch discharge pipe** ● **Connection to a back inlet gulley** ● **Connection to a soil stack**

Left: *Though the way in which the hot and cold water supplies are connected varies from machine to machine, hoses are often used at the machine end. This gives you more flexibility in your choice of site and permits easy removal for cleaning*

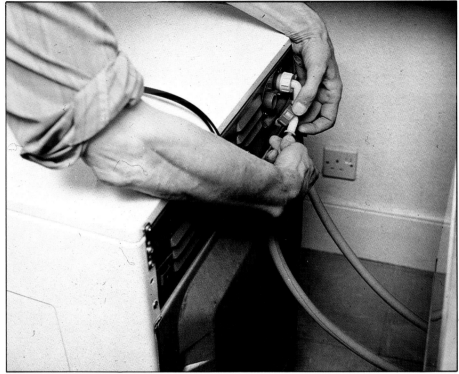

Check first!

In the UK, plumbing work is strictly controlled by local water authority by-laws. You must inform your water authority of your plans at least seven days before work starts. As well as giving practical advice, they will warn you against any possible infringement of their regulations. Work on the drainage system may need building regulations consent.

In Australia/NZ, only a licensed plumber is authorised to extend or repair any household plumbing.

Though an automatic washing machine is a boon to any household, many people are discouraged from buying one because it has to be plumbed in— both to the water supply and the drains. But providing you choose the site carefully and set about the work in a logical order, the job is not half as hard as it seems.

The work can be divided into four stages: positioning the machine; connecting up the cold water supply (probably hot, too, though many machines are cold-fill only); installing a branch discharge pipe to the drains; making the electrical connections. The last step involves plugging into a socket outlet or fitting a fused connection unit.

Choosing a site
Your first decision here is in which room to site the machine. In the UK, the choice is normally between the kitchen and bathroom, both of which have hot and cold water supplies and drainage outlets. In Australia, the

usual site is a basement utility room.

You have next to consider the type of machine, the space that will be needed around it, the existing layout of the room and the design and materials used in your plumbing system.

Of these, the plumbing system must inevitably take priority. It is no use choosing the ideal space-saving site only to find that you cannot then plumb in the machine without demolishing the house.

Drainage: In the UK, for a washing machine in a ground floor kitchen, the most suitable outlet for the discharge pipe is a back inlet gully, separated from the main discharge stack and connected to the main drain by a branch underground. This is often easier to break into than the main stack and, as it is usually there to serve the kitchen sink discharge pipe, it is likely to be in the most convenient position already.

In older houses, the sink waste sometimes discharges over an open,

trapped gully leading to the drains. You will probably be allowed to run the washing machine discharge pipe to here also, provided that the end of the pipe is below the grid.

If the pipe has to connect to the main stack, the latter will need a branch fitting. Though this is relatively easy to fit to a plastics stack, on the older, cast-iron or galvanized steel types the job is best left to an expert. Indeed, it is probably better to take the opportunity of replacing the stack with a new one. A connection to an existing hopper head may not be allowed; check with your local council's building department.

Water supply: Breaking into the hot and cold water supply generally presents less of a problem, as the final connections to the machine are usually made with flexible hose. Nevertheless, the supply must be near enough to the site to allow you to keep pipe runs as short—and as simple—as possible.

In the UK, a cold-only supply might come direct from the rising main (usually the easiest arrangement if the machine is in a kitchen), though some water authorities do not allow this.

A hot and cold fill machine is best supplied via the cold water storage cistern or tank. In this case, as with some showers, low water pressure is sometimes a problem on upper floors or in flats and bungalows. Manufacturers

1 *Having isolated and drained down the pipes, sever them with a fine toothed hacksaw. Make the cuts as cleanly as possible*

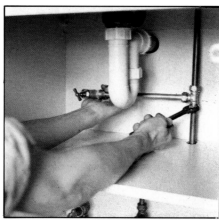

2 *With careful planning, you can keep the run simple and the number of joints to a minimum. Use compression or capillary joints*

3 *With some types of valve, the flexible hose ends may simply screw on, as here. With other types different fixings will be needed*

generally specify a minimum 'head' of water—that is, the distance from the base of the storage tank to the point where the supply enters the back of the washing machine—and you should bear this in mind when choosing a site for your machine. If you cannot meet the minimum head requirement, consult both the manufacturer and your local water authority.

In Australia, an automatic washing machine is almost always connected direct to mains pressure supply.

The pipe run must be arranged so that the branches do not cross one another, with the stop valves easily accessible. When you are planning the run, consider the best place to fit tee pieces to the supply pipes; it may be better to have a slightly longer run in order to avoid disturbing existing fixtures and fittings.

Breaking into the supply

Having chosen your supply pipes, turn off the stop valves that are nearest to them and drain off the pipes by opening the taps at the end of each pipe run. With cistern-fed supplies, if there

A. Below: *A typical completed installation. Note that in some areas, taking the cold supply direct from the rising main is not allowed*

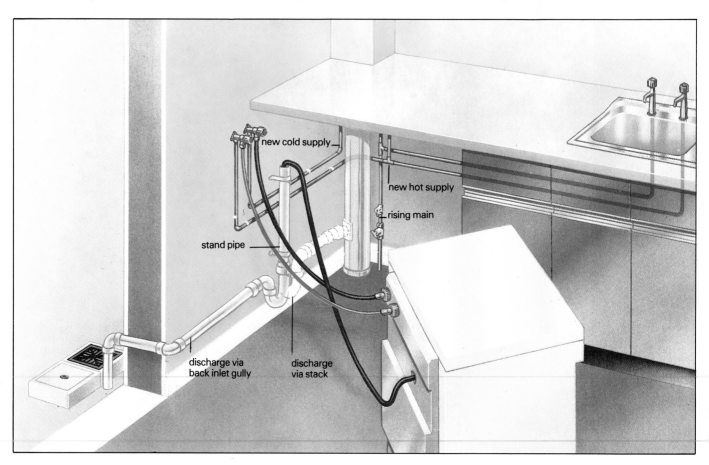

new cold supply

new hot supply

rising main

stand pipe

discharge via back inlet gully

discharge via stack

are no local valves, look for a cold supply stop valve on the pipe running out of the base of the storage tank and a hot supply valve on the cold supply pipe running into the base of the hot water cylinder.

If you still have no luck, you must tie up the ball valve on the storage tank and drain down the system. It is sensible to turn off the boiler or heat source before you turn off any water services. If you are taking the cold supply from the rising main, turn off at the mains.

To break into the supply, you must either cut out sections of pipe large enough to take tee fittings or remove and replace existing fittings. Opt for whichever gives the simpler pipe run.

Using the former method, measure and mark the cut sections very carefully against the tee fittings. Be sure to allow for the extra pipe taken up by the joints. If there is a joint already near a cut section, it may be easier to loosen this, make one cut and remove the pipe altogether (fig. 1). You can then trim it to the new length required on the bench. Make the cuts with a fine toothed hacksaw, ensuring that the pipe ends are kept square.

Having prepared the pipe ends, fit the tee pieces; you have a choice of either compression joints or capillary joints, as already mentioned on page 14.

Connecting to the machine

Somewhere between the tee pieces and the washing machine inlets, stop valves must be fitted so that the supply can be disconnected at any time. Some manufacturers provide these with their machines while others leave the choice of valve entirely up to you. Suitable fixing points for valves are normally the wall or the side of a unit.

Mark the points clearly then measure back and fit pipe runs—using 15mm copper tube in the UK—between these and the tee pieces. Where necessary, support with wall brackets every 1.2m. Fit the valve holders to the ends of the pipe runs before you fix them to the wall.

Finally, screw the valves provided into the holders and secure the flexible connections to the machine. On no account should you attempt to shorten the flexible fittings supplied with the machine: these are designed specially to length in order to balance out irregularities in the water flow.

If you are fitting your own valves, simply fit these to the ends of your pipe runs and connect them to the flexible hoses (see fig. 3). But as above, make sure that the valves are so positioned that the hoses do not cross or kink.

4 *Back inside the house, connect the waste trap for the standpipe at the point where the discharge pipe comes through the wall*

6 *Finally, when you are happy that everything is functioning as it should, make good the hole in the wall with appropriate filler*

In both cases, test the pipework and all joints for leaks at this stage.

Installing the discharge pipe

For the pipes themselves, follow the sizes and plastics type specified in the manufacturer's handbook. Most often these will be 32mm PVC linked with solvent welded joints.

Connection to a back inlet gully:
The simplest way to connect to a gully is to run the pipe just below the surface of the grid. To do this, replace the grid (if it is a metal one) with a plastics type, and cut a hole in it of the right size to take the pipe.

Alternatively, you may want to take this opportunity to replace an old gully (whether back inlet type or not) with a modern plastics back inlet gully. To

5 *Cut the standpipe to the required length, screw it to the trap and fit the support bracket. Now is the time to check the run for leaks*

7 *Roll the washing machine into place being very careful that you do not tangle the flexible hoses or press them against the wall*

do this, start by digging away the soil around the gully so that you expose the upper part (fig. B). Remove the water in the trap beside it with a plunger.

Next using an angle grinder and cutting disc, cut away enough of the pipe to accommodate your new PVC gully fitting. Bear in mind as you mark up for the cut that the new gully must finish above ground level and be far enough away from the wall to allow you the discharge pipe (fig. A). Before you sever the pipe completely, support the gully from below to take the weight of the trap.

Remove the old gully and fittings above the cut completely. Then bed a PVC-to-clay pipe adaptor over the cut end of the drain run using rapid-hardening cement; hold the adaptor in place for

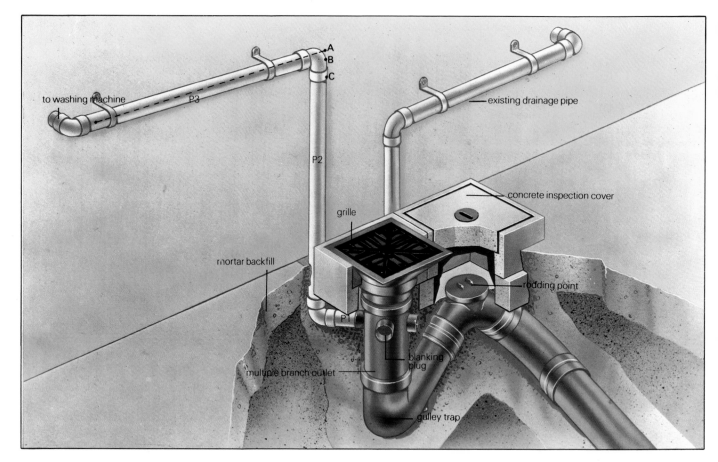

to washing machine — P3
A
B
C
existing drainage pipe
P2
concrete inspection cover
grille
rodding point
mortar backfill
blanking plug
multiple branch outlet
gulley trap

a few minutes to ensure a sound bond. Next, shovel some almost-dry concrete into the hole and bed the gully trap on it with the trap outlet fitted into the adaptor. Finally, check that the hopper fits at the required level, assemble the components after lubricating the joints and backfill round the gully with fairly dry concrete.

Connecting the discharge pipe to the back inlet may call for a little trial-and-error. Start by connecting the bend and short length of pipe P1 (see fig. A), adjusting the length of P1 so that P2 stands out from the wall the correct distance to accommodate pipe brackets. Then fit P3 and its bends, so that the fall of the pipe is between 18mm and 45mm per metre, and so that the lower bend is vertically over the bend connected to P1. Finally, cut and fix P2.

Now continue the pipe run through the wall following the same cutting and measuring sequence. Do not permanently solvent weld the joints until you have checked the run.

After the run has been fitted as far as the wall, fill in the space between the gully and the wall with a 1:3 mortar so that the concrete gully frame is held firmly in place. Finally, solvent weld the gully hopper joint and fill in the ground around the gully with a concrete mix.

Connection to a stack: Aim to run the discharge pipe to an existing branch outlet boss. If this does not have a spare outlet, then you can either fit a new multiple connector in this position, or a boss adaptor (of the type that can be fitted to an existing stack) to a length of plain stack pipe—whichever allows the discharge pipe to have sufficient fall. If you buy new components, make sure they are compatible with the existing ones—shapes and sizes vary slightly from brand to brand.

If you are connecting to an existing spare outlet, simply cut away the blanking plug and fit the new pipe in position. A boss adaptor is almost as easy to fit: consult manufacturer's instructions. A new connector is a little more tricky: the old connector will probably have to be sawn off, and the new one may not be big enough to bridge the gap. You might have enough 'slack' in the stack to take up the gap, or you may need to fit a slightly longer piece of stack pipe.

Australia/NZ: You can connect to existing drains in the same way as described above. You can even connect to a basement floor drain, as long as this is connected to a sewer or septic tank. However, do make sure that you

B. Above: *On ground floors you may want to connect the discharge pipe to a back inlet gully with a multiple branch outlet*

are complying with your local building ordinances—if you are in any doubt at all about how to connect to your drainage system, get expert help.

Final connection
At this stage, you should have run the discharge pipe through the wall and almost to the site of the machine. The final connection is made as shown in fig. A with a 'P'-trap and stand pipe fitted to the discharge pipe length. The height of the stand pipe will be specified in the machine's handbook; in most cases, the outlet hose from the machine simply hooks into the top; the air gap stops back-siphonage.

In some circumstances, you may be able to connect the machine's outlet hose to an existing trap or waste pipe without the need for a standpipe. Sink traps are now available which incorporate a special connector for a washing machine outlet hose; alternatively, a self-cutting waste connector can be attached to a convenient point on an existing waste pipe, and the outlet hose can be attached to this.

INSTALLING A TOWEL RAIL

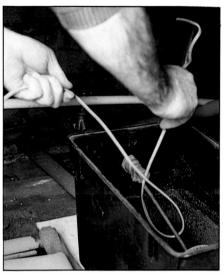

1 *Turn off the boiler, allow the system to cool down for several hours, then turn off the supply valve or tie up the cistern ball float*

● **The advantages of installing a heated towel rail** ● **The types of rail available** ● **Identifying your hot water system** ● **Making the connection to the system** ● **Installing a towel rail in an existing central heating system**

Once a luxury in its own right, the bathroom is now an area in which many householders indulge their taste for the luxurious. Yet, when they contemplate refitting the bathroom, surprisingly few people think of the one fixture that makes a really tangible contribution to bathing comfort: a heated towel rail.

If you arrange for the rail to be constantly on, then as well as providing warm dry towels at all times, the rail becomes an excellent method of fighting condensation. Quite simply, keeping the room warm prevents con-densation forming on the walls and ceilings in the first place.

Heated towel rails come in all shapes and sizes, and vary widely in their complexity. If your bathroom already contains a radiator, as part of a 'wet' central heating system, all you need do is measure it and then buy one of the clip, clamp or hang-on rails that are available. Though not heated directly, these enable you to dry and warm towels in front of the radiator without impeding its main function.

Next on the list are electric towel rails—self contained, generally oil-

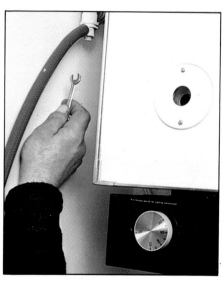

2 *Attach a hose to the lowest drain cock in the system, run it to an outside drain, open all radiator valves then open the cock*

filled, units. These come into their own where it is difficult or impossible to plumb in a hot water rail. Installing the supply for an electric towel rail is done in the same way as supplying other fixed electrical appliances in a bathroom.

But if you have a wet central heating system, whether there is a radiator in the bathroom or not, a proper hot

3 *Cut copper tubing with a pipe cutter or a hacksaw fitted with a fine toothed blade and clean up the burr with a fine file*

4 *Bend copper tubing with a pipe bender, or use a spring or rubber 'bendable core' (to stop kinks) and manipulate the tube over your knee*

5 *Locate the primary circuit flow pipe (on the side of the hot water cylinder) and cut through it along a convenient straight run*

water towel rail is well worth considering. The plain tubular sort offer plenty of towel hanging space and generally produce enough heat to keep the average size bathroom at a constantly comfortable temperature. They can be plumbed in to the house hot water system—rather than the radiator circuit—so that they remain hot even when the heating is switched off—in the summer, say. And, as most bathrooms have a hot water cylinder close at hand, this makes installation straightforward.

Some hot water rails include a radiator panel to provide extra heating facilities, but these can be fitted only to indirect type heating systems where there is no risk of them becoming clogged with scale. Tubular rails, on the other hand, can be installed in any

hot water system—direct or indirect—which incorporates a storage tank/boiler/hot water cylinder arrangement.

Identifying your water system

Before you plumb-in a hot water towel rail, it is obviously important to know what type of hot water system you have and to identify the pipes.

In the older, direct system, water heated by the boiler rises by thermal convection to the hot water cylinder. Here, it continues to rise until it passes out of the top (crown) to the hot taps, via the hot water supply pipe. Fresh water is fed to the system from the cold storage tank and enters via the base of the cylinder. From here, it sinks to the boiler under force of gravity.

If no water is drawn off the hot taps, the water in the system continues to circulate between the cylinder and the boiler. When hot water is used, fresh water is taken in and heated to the desired temperature.

Although simple, the main drawback of the direct system is scale. This is released every time fresh water is heated above about 60°C and clogs cylinder and boiler pipework alike. In the indirect system—most often found with central heating—the problem of scale is avoided by having two separate circuits. The first—known as the primary circuit—runs continuously between the boiler and cylinder. The water in it is always hot, but because it is never drawn off it is introduced fresh only once. Consequently, it releases its scale the first time it is heated and from then onwards it is relatively scale-free.

The hot water cylinder in an indirect system contains a loop—the

heat exchanger—through which the hot primary circuit water passes. As it does so, it transfers its heat to fresh water fed to the base of the cylinder from the cold storage tank. This fresh water then becomes hot—but not hot enough to release scale—and rises out of the crown of the cylinder to feed the hot taps in the normal way. The cold feed, the outer part of the cylinder and the pipework supplying the hot taps comprise what is known as the secondary circuit.

Both direct and indirect systems contain vent pipes to guard against the build-up of excessive pressure. The direct system has a single vent pipe, rising from the crown of the cylinder, or the hot tap supply pipe, to above the cold storage tank. The indirect system has this pipe too, plus another rising from the primary circuit flow pipe to above the expansion tank.

The function of the expansion tank in an indirect system is to top up the water in the primary circuit, should some be lost by leakage or evaporation, and to allow for the slight expansion of the water as it is heated. The flow in the primary circuit may be by gravity—as in the direct system—or included in the radiator circuit and under pump pressure. In the latter case, a motorized valve distributes water from the boiler between the cylinder heat exchanger and the radiators as and where it is required.

Making the connection

Hot water towel rails work on the same principle as radiators, with two connection points for flow and return pipes. In both direct and indirect systems, pipes can run from these to intercept the hot water flow pipe between the boiler and the hot water cylinder. This pipe is cut, and T-shaped connectors inserted to make the final connections (fig. 6).

Obviously, it is absolutely essential to know which pipes are which before you connect to them. This may call for a bit of detective work—particularly in the case of an indirect system—before you go any further. But in any case you should aim to make the connections somewhere around the hot water cylinder. Here, the pipes are easier to identify.

Direct systems: Most direct cylinders have four pipes running from them (fig. B). Of the two near the crown, the lower is the flow pipe from the boiler which supplies the cylinder with hot water. The other is the hot water supply pipe, which supplies the hot taps and generally also holds the

Making the connection

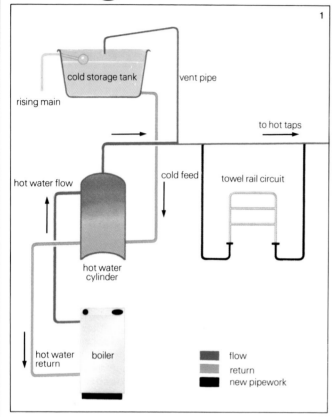

rising main

cold storage tank

vent pipe

to hot taps

hot water flow

cold feed

towel rail circuit

hot water cylinder

hot water return

boiler

flow
return
new pipework

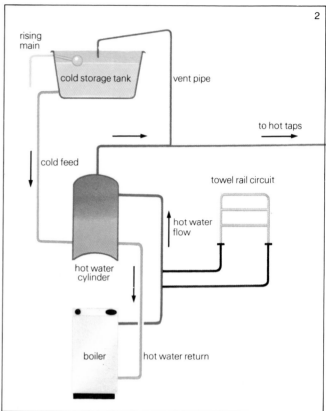

rising main

cold storage tank

vent pipe

to hot taps

cold feed

hot water flow

towel rail circuit

hot water cylinder

boiler

hot water return

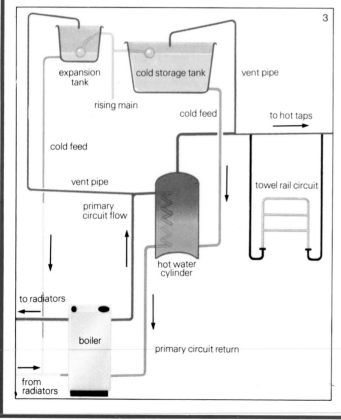

expansion tank

cold storage tank

vent pipe

rising main

cold feed

to hot taps

cold feed

vent pipe

primary circuit flow

towel rail circuit

hot water cylinder

to radiators

boiler

primary circuit return

from radiators

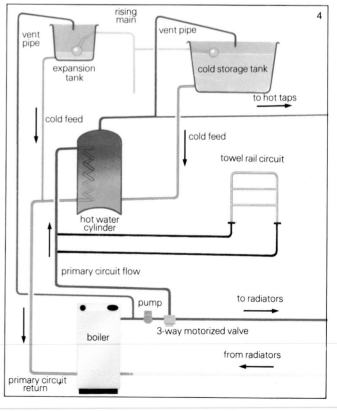

rising main

vent pipe

vent pipe

expansion tank

cold storage tank

to hot taps

cold feed

cold feed

towel rail circuit

hot water cylinder

primary circuit flow

pump

to radiators

boiler

3-way motorized valve

primary circuit return

from radiators

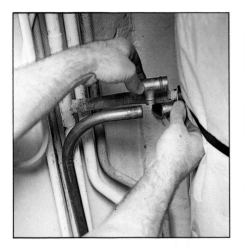

6 *To take off the hot water you must insert T-connectors into the flow pipe. You can use either compression or capillary fittings*

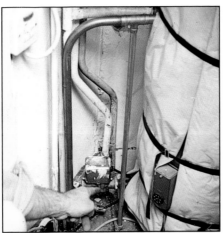

7 *Fix the T-connectors in place, then run copper tubing from the site of the heated towel rail back to the cylinder and join it up*

8 *In the case of a solid floor, bury the piping in a channel 100mm deep. The pipe must be protected with a suitable insulating cover*

vent pipe. In some cases, the vent rises directly from the cylinder (in which case there will be a total of five pipe connections).

Of the two near the base, one is the cold feed from the cold storage tank and the other is the return taking back cooled water to the boiler.

Indirect system: Indirect cylinders have the same hot supply vent pipe at the crown and cold feed at the base as direct ones. But the primary flow and return pipes to and from the boiler generally run into the side of the cylinder and stand out from the rest of the pipework. An additional complication is the primary circuit vent pipe. This may pass near the water cylinder, or it may be connected to the flow pipe.

About the only safe way to identify

9 *Mark the position of the towel rail fixing holes on the wall and floor, then drill them with a masonry bit and insert wall plugs*

10 *Secure the towel rail in place with the screws provided, but do not tighten the screws until each one has been started*

Left: *A direct central heating system* **(1)** *has a single circuit in which the heated water is shared by the radiators and hot taps. Installing the towel rail circuit in the feed to the hot taps means that it works only when hot water is being taken (for example, at bathtime). Installing the towel rail in the hot water feed to the storage cylinder* **(2)** *gives it a constant supply of hot water and is more satisfactory. An indirect central heating system* **(3)** *has two circuits in which the water heated for the radiators is separate from the hot water circuit. The towel rail may be inserted in the hot water circuit (as in* **(1)**)*, or* **(4)** *in the primary flow circuit which allows it to be controlled independently of both the radiators and the hot water taps for greater flexibility*

the pipes is to trace each one in turn and then label it clearly somewhere near the connection point. Once you have the found the flow and return to the boiler, search for a suitable interception point on the flow pipe. This should preferably be on a straight, horizontal run. Make sure, too, that there will be room to work and that the pipe route to the rail will not be too tortuous.

Installation

Once you have decided on a site for the rail and identified the connection points, you are ready to begin installation. On all types of hot water system, the first job is to turn off the boiler and allow both pipes and cylinder to cool down. What you do next depends on the type of system.

Direct system: In this case it is preferable to turn off the cold water supply at the cold storage tank—rather than at the rising main—so that you will still have use of the kitchen cold tap. If there is no stop valve, tie up the ball valve in the closed position (fig. 1).

Drain the cold tank by opening all taps fed from it, then drain down the hot water system. Attach a hose to the drain cock, which should be located adjacent to the boiler in the return pipe, and having placed the other end of the hose at a suitable drainage point, open the cock.

With the cylinder empty, the hot water flow pipes can be cut using a fine toothed hacksaw and the T-shaped fittings connected. Since only one radiator/rail is to be served, the pipe

11 *Smear jointing compound on the threads of the towel rail connecting sockets before you screw on the wheel and lockshield valves*

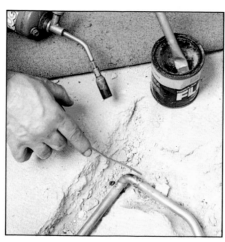

12 *Route the copper piping into place then secure all the joints to complete the circuit. Try to use capillary fittings where you can*

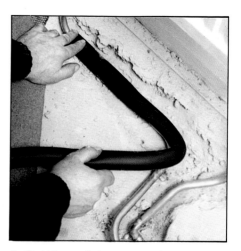

13 *When all the connections have been made, you must clad the piping for protection where it passes through walls or floors*

14 *Turn on the water supply and allow the system to fill up. Check for any leaks, then make good with a cement/sharp sand mortar mix*

15 *Finally you must bleed each radiator in the system in order to expel any air which may have found its way into it*

runs from the teeing points to the site of the unit can usually be of 15mm copper tube.

Assuming that the bathroom is on the first floor, and the floor itself is a conventional joist and board structure, the pipes should run by the shortest possible route under the floorboards. If they must run across joists, notch them into the tops of the joists, resting them on small pads of pipe insulation. Where changes of direction are necessary, use elbow compression fittings or bend the pipe with a bending spring.

If running the pipes under the floor is not feasible, soldered capillary fittings are less obtrusive—and cheaper—than the compression type. Where changes of direction are necessary in surface piping, bend the pipe in

preference to using bulky ready-made fittings for a neater finish.

If the bathroom is on a solid ground floor, it may be possible to run the pipes in the ceiling void, then down to connect to the towel rail. The connections to the rail are made with normal radiator valve fittings, a wheel valve with a turnable head on the flow (hot supply) side, and a lockshield valve with a screw-fixed cap on the return side. These compression-joint to the pipes, which must be cut to length once the rail is in place.

Unlike radiators, which are usually hung on brackets fixed to the wall, towel rails—including those incorporating radiator panels—are fixed to the floor by screws passing through their flanged feet. Some also have flanges at the top so that you can fix

them to the wall for added stability.

With the unit fixed and the connections made, check that all taps and drain cocks are closed, open the air vent—normally located under the top rail of a towel rail—and restore the water supply. As the system fills, watch for water appearing at the rail vent. When it does so, close the vent, restart the boiler and run it for about half an hour. Then re-open the vent to release any trapped air in the towel rail itself, with a small pot under the valve to catch any water.

Indirect systems: Here, there is no need to shut off the water at the main cold storage tank or drain the hot water cylinder. Instead, cut off the supply to the expansion tank, attach a hose to the central heating system drain cock—which should be located on the boiler return pipe at its lowest point—and open the cock.

The water in the system should contain rust-inhibiting chemicals, and you may feel it worth collecting the drained water in containers to be put back into the system when you refill it rather than buy a new supply.

Having drained the system completely, proceed as for a direct hot water system. When the installation is complete, refill the system by restoring the cold supply at the expansion tank. After filling, turn all your radiator valves to the fully open position and bleed the radiators in turn to remove airlocks. When you are opening lockshield valves, count how many turns it takes, and afterwards close them by the same number. You may find that the system needs further bleeding after several days, but this is perfectly normal.

CURING A DRIPPING TAP

Dripping taps are a source of constant irritation for any household. But for a repair as small as mending a leaking tap, calling in a plumber is an expensive proposition

Since the leak is usually caused by a worn-out or perished washer, one way of solving the problem is to replace the whole tap with a new one of the non-drip, washer-less type. A far cheaper way is to learn to mend the tap yourself. Replacement parts cost only pennies and can usually be fitted in a few minutes, once you know how to take the tap apart.

How taps work

Most taps which have washers work in the same basic way: turning the handle raises or lowers a spindle with the rubber or nylon washer on the end in its seating. When the spindle is raised water flows through the seating and out of the spout; when it is lowered, the flow is cut off. But when the washer becomes worn and disintegrates, water can still creep through, irrespective of the position of the spindle. This is what usually causes the tap to drip. If the seals around the moving spindle are worn as well, leaks will also appear around the handle and the outer cover. Because you will have to dismantle the tap to replace either the washer or the seals, it is usually worth doing both jobs at the same time. If fitting new ones fails to cure the drips, the washer seating itself is probably worn. This is a common problem with older taps, and the cure is to regrind the tap seat or fit a plastic seat on top.

The most common type of household tap is the upright *pillar tap* (fig. A). The *bib-tap* (fig. B) is similar in operation, but fits into the wall above an appliance or on an outside wall. The patented Supatap is a British type of bib-tap incorporating a valve which enables you to complete repairs without having to turn off the water supply. Modern baths and sink units often have a mixer tap with a fixed or a swivelling nozzle. This is really two pillar taps combined and they are repaired in the same way.

Replacing a washer

To replace the washer on a conventional type of tap, start by turning off the water supply. In Australia, use the mains supply tap next to the water meter. It is vital not to leave the supply off for more than a few hours if you have a mains supply water heater. Then turn the tap you are repairing on fully to drain away any water left in the pipe. Put the plug in to prevent any of the tap com-

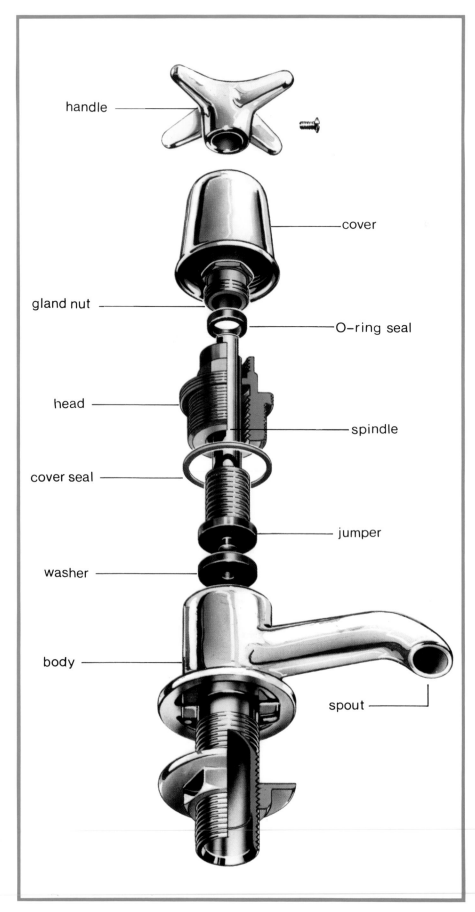

handle

cover

gland nut

O-ring seal

head

spindle

cover seal

jumper

washer

body

spout

ponents slipping down the plug-hole.

The assembly which holds the tap washer and the spindle is known as the head. On older taps, it is covered by an outer shield which screws into the tap body. Newer taps have a combined shield and handle which must be removed as one unit.

To remove a conventional shield, make sure that the tap is turned fully on. Loosen the shield with a spanner or a wrench, unscrew it and leave it loose. You can avoid damaging the chrome plating by covering the jaws of whichever tool you are using with a piece of rag.

Modern shield/handles are either simply a push-fit on to the spindle or else are secured in place by a screw through the top. Check the former first by gently pulling the handle upwards (fig. B on page 29).

If it stays fast, dig out the plastic cover in the top to expose the securing screw. With this removed, the handle can be pulled off (fig. 1 on page 30).

The next stage is to remove the head. Locate the hexagon nut at the bottom of the assembly and loosen it, again using the wrench or spanner. Unscrew the head from the body of the tap and remove it. At the base, you can see the washer (or what remains of it) seated on its *jumper*.

On older taps the head assembly will be made of brass and the washer will be held on the jumper by a small nut. Loosen this with the pliers, remove the old pieces of washer and put on the new one, maker's name against the jumper.

On newer taps, the entire head is made of nylon and the washer and jumper are combined in one replaceable unit which slots into the bottom of the assembly. To replace the washer, you simply pull out the old jumper and push in the new one.

Once you have fitted the new washer, you can re-assemble the tap and turn the water supply back on. If the new washer is seated correctly, there will be no drips from the nozzle and you should be able to turn the tap on and off with little effort.

Supataps
When replacing a washer in a Supatap, there is no need to turn off the water supply—this is done automatically by the check-valve inside the tap. To gain access to the washer, hold the

A. *Exploded view of a typical pillar tap showing its components. On older types the washer may be bolted to the jumper plate*

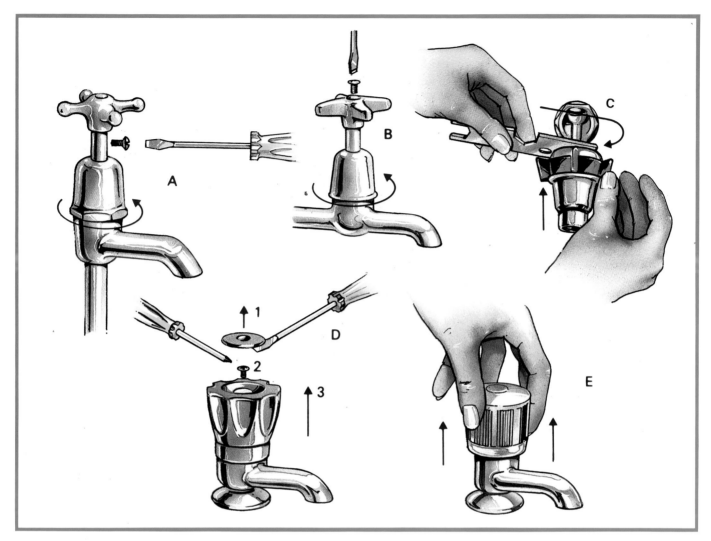

handle in one hand while you loosen the gland nut above it with the other. Holding the gland nut and turning in an anticlockwise direction, unscrew the handle from the tap. As you do this, there will be a slight rush of water which will stop as soon as the handle is removed and the check-valve drops down.

Protruding from the dismantled handle, you will see the tip of the flow straightener. Push or knock this out on to a table and identify the push-in washer/jumper assembly at one end. Pull off the old washer/jumper and replace it with a new one. Before you re-assemble the tap it is a good idea to clean the flow straightener with a nail brush.

Stop-valve taps
There is normally little difference between a crutch-type stop-valve tap and the more conventional type of pillar tap. However, you should remember, in addition to turning off the main supply to the valve, to

also turn on any outlets controlled by it. This will drain any water left in the pipe to which the valve has been fitted and minimize the risk of creating an airlock.

Normally, stop-valve taps have no outer shield and the head is exposed. Loosen the nut securing it with a spanner or wrench and then unscrew the head to expose the washer assembly. Stop-valve washers are usually held in their jumpers with a small retaining nut like the older type of pillar tap described above.

Leaking spindles
If the leak is coming from around the spindle of the tap rather than the nozzle there are two possible causes. Either the O-ring seal around the spindle has worn out or else the gland nut which holds it is in need of adjustment. Both problems tend to be more common on older taps with brass heads: the newer sort with nylon heads have a better record for remaining watertight.

B. *Designs of washer-type taps vary widely, but dismantling procedures will follow one of these: a) old pillar tap, b) old bib tap, c) Supatap, d) and e) new-style pillar taps*

To service the spindle, you have to remove the tap handle. On newer types of tap, this may have been done already in order to replace the washer, but on older cross-head taps the handle will still be in place.

The cross-head will be held on either by a grub screw in the side or by a screw through the top, possibly obscured by a plastic cover. Having undone the screw, you should be able to pull off the handle. If it will not move, turn the tap fully off and unscrew the shield below to force the handle loose.

Once you have done this, mark the position of the gland nut at the top of the tap head against the head itself with a screwdriver. Next loosen the nut and unscrew it completely. Check the condition of the O-ring

1 On this type of tap, remove the cover to expose the securing screw. Undo this and pull the loosened handle upwards to expose the spindle

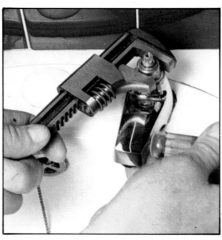

2 When you undo the locking nut, try to wedge the body of the tap against the nearest firm support to avoid undue strain on the pipe

3 Unscrew the head assembly to get at the washer. Check the seating in the tap body for corrosion while the tap is dismantled

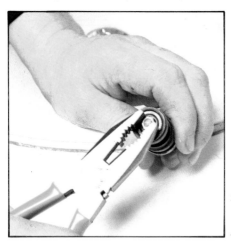

4 On some types of tap, the washer is held to its jumper by a small securing nut on the base of the head—undo this with pliers

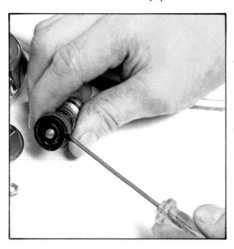

5 You can then dig out the old washer and replace it. For a temporary repair you can reverse the old washer

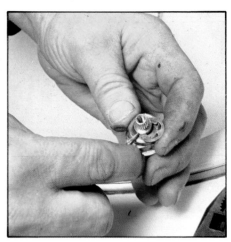

6 To replace the spindle O-ring seals, dig out the circlip holding the spindle to the tap head. Take care not to damage the circlip

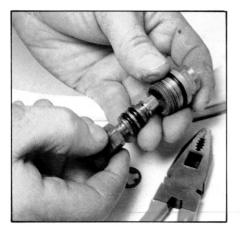

7 Once the circlip is loosened, you can slide the spindle out. You can see the various O-rings used on this particular design

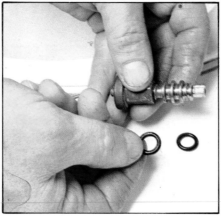

8 If the seals are worn, prise them off with a pin. Slide on new ones and make sure these are properly seated before re-assembling the tap

9 To replace a Supatap washer, start by loosening the locknut above the nozzle assembly. There is no need to turn off the water supply

or packing around the seating below and, where necessary, replace it. If an O-ring is not available, use string smeared with petroleum jelly.

If the seal around the spindle appears to be in good condition, the leak is probably due to the gland nut above working loose. Replace the nut and tighten it gently so that it just passes the mark that you made against the head. Temporarily replace the handle and check that the tap can be easily turned. If it is too tight, slacken the gland nut. But if, with the water supply turned on, the tap instead continues to leak, then the gland nut will require further tightening to solve the problem.

Taps without gland nuts
Some taps do not have conventional gland nut assemblies, even though their heads are made of brass. Instead, the spindle is held in the head by means of a circlip (snap ring). The seal between them is provided by two or more O-rings around the spindle body, and if these are worn they must be replaced. Follow the procedures above for removing the tap handle and unscrewing the head. Dig out the circlip around the top of the spindle as shown in fig. 6 and you will find that the spindle drops out. The O-rings around it can then be rolled off and replaced.

Leaking swivel nozzles
Mixer taps with swivelling spouts are often prone to leaks around the base of the spout itself, caused by the seals in the base wearing out. Providing you are working on the spout alone, it will not be necessary to turn off the water. Start by loosening the shroud around the base, which will either screw on or else be secured by a small grub screw at the back.

Around the spout, inside the base, you will find a large circlip (snap ring). Pinch this together with the pliers and remove it, then pull out the spout.

Dig the worn seals out of the exposed base and discard them. Fit the new ones around the spout: if you fit them into the base, you will have great difficulty in getting the spout to go back in the correct position. With the seals around the spout it should slot in easily and you can then replace the circlip and the shroud.

If you have to make a temporary repair to a tap seating—necessary if dripping continues even when the washer has been replaced—use a new plastic washer and seating kit.

10 *The flow straightener can be knocked out using light taps from a hammer. The washer and its jumper are on the other end*

11 *The combined washer and jumper is prised from the flow straightener and a new one of the same size slotted in its place*

12 *To cure a leaking nozzle, undo the shroud at the base. This either unscrews or may be released by a grub screw at the back*

13 *Pinch together the large circlip at the base. Use pliers for this and take care not to scratch the chromed finish of the nozzle*

14 *Pull the spout from its seat and then dig out the worn seal in the exposed base. Remove all bits before fitting new ones*

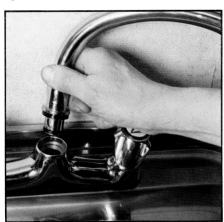

15 *Place the replacement seal on the spout before refitting this. Replace the circlip and then screw on the shroud*

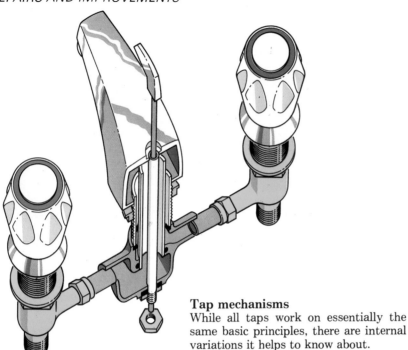

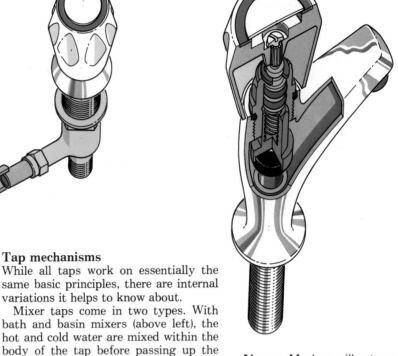

Above: *Three-hole mixer taps for basins and bidets have the body of the tap concealed below the surface of the appliance*

Below: *Kitchen mixers take their cold water supplies direct from the rising main; mixing takes place as water leaves the spout*

Tap mechanisms

While all taps work on essentially the same basic principles, there are internal variations it helps to know about.

Mixer taps come in two types. With bath and basin mixers (above left), the hot and cold water are mixed within the body of the tap before passing up the spout.

Pillar taps operate by screwing the washer down onto the tap seating; with Supataps, opening the tap allows the washer to drop away from the seating.

Above: *Modern pillar taps usually have O-rings instead of old-fashioned hemp packing. Ceramic discs are beginning to replace the washer mechanism on some taps; these need little maintenance*

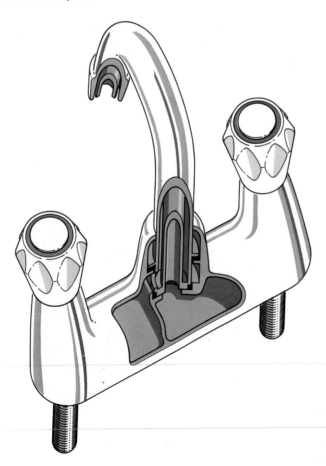

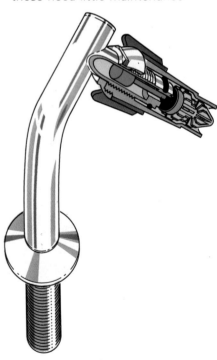

Above: *The Supatap is still the only type of tap that can be rewashered without the need to turn off the water supply first. They are available with different pillar heights for sink and basin use*

MAINTAINING CENTRAL HEATING

Left: *All the radiators in a central heating system should be bled of air once or twice a year. If there is a substantial air lock in a radiator, it will prevent it from functioning normally*

Maintenance of the system

Although all central heating systems should be serviced at least once a year by qualified engineers, you can keep the system running reliably by correct use and regular maintenance.

It is not advisable to switch off heating at night during cold weather. A small amount of heat—to ensure that the temperature throughout the

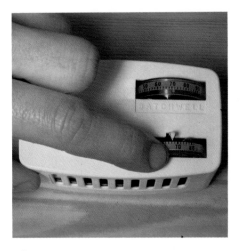

1 *To check a room thermostat, turn it to its lowest setting. Turn it back up again, listening for a click as the pump is switched on*

Operating your system for maximum efficiency
● Regular maintenance ● Troubleshooting checks ● Dealing with noise ● Draining the system ● Clearing airlocks

When a central heating system ceases to function properly, it becomes an expensive liability. But it does not always take an expert to repair it. Many common faults can be cured just as easily by the householder.

The most complicated part of the average domestic central heating system is the boiler itself. This may require specialist knowledge and tools to put it right should it fail—but failures in boilers which are regularly serviced are rare. More prone to trouble are circulation pumps, thermostats and radiators which only have a limited life.

Faults here are usually easy to identify and even if a specialist has to be called in, being able to pinpoint a problem will help keep repair bills to a minimum.

Wet central heating systems

In order to identify a particular fault in a central heating system, it is worth having some idea of how the system works. Older systems may be directly linked to the hot water boiler, but now indirect installations are the norm.

In most modern systems, hot water flows from the boiler to the radiators and hot water cylinder, releases its heat and returns to be reheated. The flow is created artificially by an electric circulation pump which is normally mounted adjacent to the boiler. The pump is controlled by a time clock and, in most cases, by a room thermostat as well.

At pre-selected times, the mechanism in the clock switches on the pump. The pump then sends hot water to the radiators, heating the house.

2 *To find out whether a circulation pump is working, hold one end of a screwdriver against the casing with the handle to your ear*

house never falls below 10°C (50°F)—cuts the time needed to reach full operating temperature and may, in the long run, save fuel. It will also help to reduce condensation and prevent frost damage to the system.

The boiler should never be run at too low a thermostat setting. There is no economic advantage to be gained and it can shorten the life of the boiler. The boiler thermostat in a conventional small bore system should be set at up to 82°C (180°F) in winter. In summer, when the system is required for hot water only, it should be kept at not less than 54°C (130°F).

If the system is oil-fired, the oil tank should be examined annually. Any external rust should be removed with a wire brush and glasspaper and then painted over with black bitumen paint. Keep the vent pipe on top of the tank

clear, removing any obstruction with a stiff piece of wire. A piece of fine wire mesh can be fitted over the end of the vent pipe to ensure that leaves do not enter the tank and restrict the flow of fuel to the boiler.

To clean the oil filter on an oil tank, turn off the stop cock and remove the filter bowl. Clean the element with paraffin, dry it and refit. At the same time check the oil line from the tank to the boiler for leaks, tightening joints where necessary.

When a solid fuel boiler is not in use it should be left clean. Remove sooty deposits from the combustion chamber and flue and leave the damper and boiler doors open to allow a current of air to pass through. Have the flue cleaned at least once a year.

If a central heating system has to be left drained for any length of time

and stop valves are fitted on either side of the circulation pump, you can close the valves, remove the pump and dry it thoroughly to prevent rusting.

Once or twice a year, the circulation pump valves and all the radiator valves should be turned as far as they will go in both directions and then back to their original setting. This will prevent them becoming fixed.

Overheating

Overheating is one of the most common faults found in wet central heating systems. In all cases of overheating, if the fault cannot be rectified at once, the supply of gas or oil to the boiler should be cut off as a precaution. If you can run the circulation pump with the boiler off, keep it circulating water so that the heat is dissipated through the radiators. With

3 On pumps with all-metal casings, you may have to drain the system and remove the unit before you can unscrew the casing

4 If the rotor has seized, you may be able to free it by inserting a screwdriver into one of the slots and levering gently

5 To free an air lock in the pump, unscrew the vent valve located at the top. When water begins to trickle out, close the valve

6 To check the boiler thermostat, turn the dial down and then back to its maximum setting. If there is no click, the thermostat is jammed

If the sender bulb on the end of the copper capillary has come out of place, reposition it and replace its securing clip

7 If the sender bulb on the end of the copper capillary has come out of place, reposition it and replace its securing clip

8 Make sure that the level of water in the expansion tank is not more than 150mm below the valve outlet. If it is, add more water

a solid fuel boiler, rake the fire into the ashpan and remove it.

If the house feels abnormally hot, check the time clock and, if there is one, the room thermostat. These may be failing to turn the pump off when they should or have had their settings accidentally advanced. Start by turning the time clock down to the present setting. If the radiators do not cool down at the time they are supposed to, the mechanism of the clock has probably jammed and will have to be replaced with a new one.

To check a room thermostat, turn it down to its lowest setting and then back up again. A click should be heard as the switch inside turns the pump on. If there is no click, the unit will have to be replaced.

If the whole system is overheating seriously, the radiator pipes may make prolonged knocking or hissing noises and there will be excessive temperature in the boiler delivery pipe. One possible reason for this is failure of the circulation pump.

To find out whether the pump is working, hold one end of a screwdriver against the casing with the other end to your ear and listen for the hum of the rotor inside (fig. 2): if there is no noise, this is probably stuck. On pumps with a screw-on glass inspection cover, the rotor can be freed quite easily. Turn the pump off, unscrew the cover and insert a screwdriver into one of the slots in the rotor. If the rotor does not spin freely, it should be possible to free it by levering gently with the screwdriver (fig. 4).

On pumps which have all metal casings, the water supply must be cut off before opening the cover. In most cases, there are stop valves on each side for this purpose but where no such valves are fitted, the system will have to be drained before carrying out any work on the pump.

If the pump is heard to be working but water is evidently not circulating, there is probably an air lock. At the top of the pump you will find a vent valve—operated either by a key or a screwdriver—from which the pump can be bled (fig. 5).

To do this, turn the pump off and leave it for a few hours to allow the water in the system to settle. Then open the valve to bleed the air off. A hiss of air will be followed by a trickle of water: when the trickle becomes constant, close the valve.

If the fault is not in the pump, the boiler thermostat may have failed. The thermostat, a small box with a dial on the top, is located behind the boiler casing. Remove the casing and check

that the electrical connections on the thermostat are sound. Check also that the sender bulb on the end of the copper capillary from the thermostat to the boiler has not fallen out of its socket (fig. 7). If so reposition it and replace the securing clip.

Note the setting on the boiler thermostat dial and turn it down low. After a few minutes turn it back towards its maximum setting and listen for a click. If there is no click, it may mean that the thermostat has jammed and you should call in a qualified engineer to check it.

If the boiler thermostat appears to be working, check to see whether the boiler flue outlet outside has become blocked in some way. Depending on the nature of the blockage, expert help may be needed in order to clear it.

If the flue is free of any obstruction, the next thing to check is the expansion tank. The ball valve supplying it may have become jammed or seized, in which case there may not be enough water in the system to absorb the heating action of the boiler. If the level in the tank is more than 150mm from the valve outlet, free the valve and introduce more water into the system. Where the valve is completely seized, replace it with a new ballcock, arm and piston unit.

Central heating too cool

If all the radiators are cool and the boiler is working correctly, the fault probably lies with one of the thermostats, the time clock or the circulation pump. Carry out checks outlined above under 'Overheating', paying special attention to the position of a room thermostat if fitted. This reacts to the temperature around it, and a nearby heat source can cause it to give a false reading even though the mechanism may be perfectly sound.

To work efficiently, the thermostat should be mounted on an internal wall at least 1.5m above the floor and away from draughts, radiators and direct sunlight. It should not be placed in rooms which are in constant use—such as lounges—because people generate extra heat, nor in kitchens, because of the heat from cooking and appliances. However, it should be accessible so that changes in setting can be made conveniently.

Draining the system

Before doing any major repairs or modifications to your central heating, you will have to drain, or partially drain the system. Start by turning the boiler off and leaving the system for a few hours to cool down. Turn off the

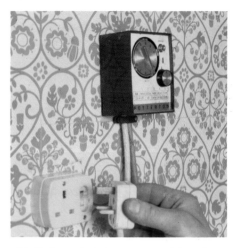

9 *Before draining a central heating system, turn off the electricity supply to the time clock and also to the immersion heater, if fitted*

10 *To shut off the water supply to the boiler, close the stop valve tap on the pipe which leads into the expansion tank*

electricity supply to the time clock and the immersion heater—if the system includes one (fig. 9).

Shut off the water supply to the boiler by closing the stop valve on the pipe into the expansion tank (fig. 10). If no stop valve is fitted, lash the ball valve in the expansion tank to a piece of wood laid across the tank.

When the system has cooled, return to the boiler and identify the main drain cock. This is usually at the front end of the boiler near the pump where it is always built into the lowest pipe. Alternatively, it may be found on a ground floor radiator. Attach one end of a garden hose to the nozzle and run the other to an outside drain. Open the drain cock by turning the nut beneath with a spanner or adjustable wrench and allow as much water as you require to drain away (fig. 12).

11 *When the system has cooled down, attach one end of a garden hose to the nozzle of the main drain cock on the boiler*

12 *Run the other end of the hose to an outside drain, then open the drain cock by turning the nut beneath with an adjustable wrench*

Refilling the system
Before refilling, close the main drain cock securely. Open the valve on the pipe leading to the expansion tank, or untie the ball valve, to admit fresh water into the system. Regulate the position of the valve so that the tank fills slowly—keeping the risk of air locks to a minimum. Also check the drain cock for leaks.

Noise
Noise is another common problem with wet central heating systems. Creaking under the floorboards and around radiators is caused by pipes—which expand and contract according to the temperature of the water—rubbing against the floor joists on which they rest. Creaking can also occur where a pipe rises through the floorboards to feed a radiator.

The creaking can often be reduced by turning the boiler thermostat down so that the radiators remain switched on for longer periods instead of constantly heating up and cooling down.

If the noise persists, take up the floorboards around the suspect area. Eventually you will find a point where one or two pipes cross a joist and are notched into the woodwork. If the notch is so small that it causes the pipes to rub against each other, enlarge it to give a better clearance. Make sure, though, that the notch does not exceed one sixth of the depth of the joist or it will seriously weaken the timber. Use a piece of rubber pipe lagging, felt or carpet, trimmed to the approximate size of the notch, to cushion the pipes (fig. 13).

Where a pipe rises through a gap in a floorboard, either enlarge the gap by filing it away or pack the space around the pipe with padding (fig. 14). Metal pipe brackets—another common source of noise—can be bent back slightly, and stuffed with felt to prevent them making direct contact with the pipes (fig. 15).

Creaking behind radiators is usually caused by the hooks on the back of the panels rubbing against their corresponding wall brackets. For serious cases, on smaller radiators, special nylon brackets can be fitted in place of the normal pressed steel type. A simpler solution is to place pieces of felt or butyl (rubber) between each hook and bracket. This can be done, with the help of an assistant, by gently lifting the radiator away from its brackets, slipping the pieces of felt into the hooks and then replacing it.

Immersion heaters
In many systems, hot water for sinks and baths is heated by a thermostatically controlled immersion heater in addition to the boiler-fed heat exchanger in the cylinder. The thermostat is pre-set to turn the heating element off when the water reaches the selected temperature. If the water is unbearably hot, the thermostat may simply need adjusting.

The thermostat control is found at the top or on the side of the hot water cylinder (fig. 16). To adjust it, turn off the electricity supply to the heater then unscrew the element cover where you will find a small dial marked centigrade, fahrenheit, or both. By hand, or with a screwdriver, turn the regulator screw to the desired temperature—normally 60°C (140°F) in hard water areas or 80°C (180°F) in those with especially soft water.

If the water heats up slowly, or the

13 *Pipes often creak where they run through a notch in a floor joist. Cushion the pipes with felt or carpet to stop the noise*

14 *A pipe may rub against wood where it rises through the floor. Pack the gap round the pipe with pieces of suitable padding*

15 *Metal pipe brackets are another common source of noise. Bend them back slightly and stuff pieces of felt into the gaps*

hot tap cools too quickly, check that the cylinder is sufficiently lagged and that the lagging is in good condition. If it is, try adjusting the thermostat. When water fails to heat up at all, either the thermostat control or the heating element are defective and will have to be replaced.

Radiator controls

Most radiators are fitted with two valves—a *handwheel* and a *lockshield* valve. The handwheel allows radiators to be shut down individually or the temperature of a radiator to be reduced by restricting the flow of water. The lockshield valve is set when the system is installed, to give a balanced flow of water through the radiator.

There is no basic difference between the two valves except that the lock-shield valve is locked into position to prevent casual adjustment. A lock-shield valve should normally need adjusting only when a radiator has to be removed for decoration or repair. When this is necessary, both the lock-shield valve and the handwheel should be closed. To close a lockshield valve, unscrew the cover and turn the valve with a spanner or a wrench.

In some cases, thermostatic radiator valves are fitted in place of hand-wheels. A radiator thermostat can be pre-set to maintain any desired temperature and is controlled by temperature sensitive bellows. As the water temperature falls, the bellows contract to allow more hot water into the radiator. Radiator thermostats are usually only suitable for use in a two-pipe system.

Above: *Most radiators are fitted with two valves, called a handwheel and a lockshield valve, which control the flow of water. The vent valve at the top is opened to release air*

Bleeding a radiator

When air accidentally enters a wet central heating system, it can find its way to a radiator and prevent this from functioning efficiently. All radiators should be bled of air once or twice a year to clear the small amounts that inevitably get into the system. But if a radiator becomes cold whilst others are functioning normally, the cause is probably a substantial air lock and the radiator should be bled immediately. The top of a radiator remaining cold while the bottom is scalding also suggests an air lock.

On most radiators a square ended hollow key—obtainable from iron-mongers—is needed to open the air vent valve at the top. To prevent air being sucked into the system, turn down the room thermostat and switch off the time clock so that the pump stops working.

Place a towel underneath the radiator to catch any drips, then open the valve by turning the key anticlock-wise until a hiss of escaping air is heard. As soon as water begins to flow, re-tighten the valve.

If air locks occur frequently in a certain radiator, you can fit a screw bleed valve or an automatic air eliminator. These save you from constantly having to bleed it by hand.

16 *To adjust the thermostat control of an immersion heater, unscrew the element cover on the top or side of the cylinder*

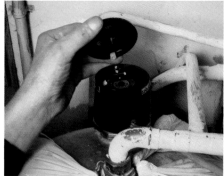

17 *Remove the cover to locate the temperature dial. Turn the dial by hand or with a screwdriver to the desired temperature mark*

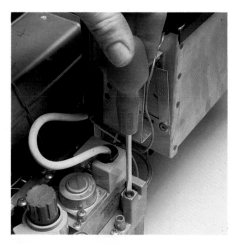

18 *If the pilot light is too small, it will keep going out. Adjust its size by turning the small screw on the gas valve with a screwdriver*

19 *If adjustment makes no difference, remove the main burner assembly and clean the pilot flame nozzle with a wire pricker*

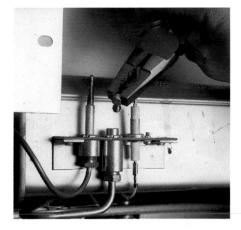

20 *If the pilot flame nozzle shows any signs of wear or has been damaged, unscrew it carefully and fit a replacement*

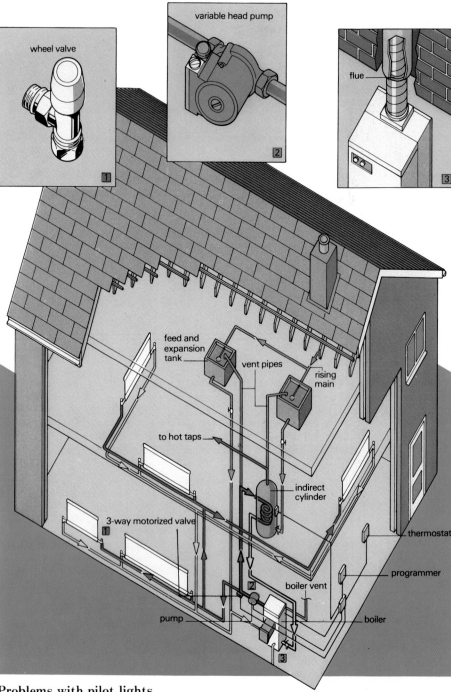

Above: *A conventional wet central heating system needs regular maintenance and good controls*

Problems with pilot lights

On gas boilers, the pilot light is intended to light the main burners when gas is released by the automatic valve. To prevent gas release when the pilot is out, a fail-safe device called a thermocouple is incorporated into the valve. The pilot flame heats its tip sufficiently to produce a tiny electrical current which then causes the gas valve to open.

If the pilot flame is too small to heat the thermocouple properly, the boiler will keep going out. The problem can be put right by adjusting the flame size (fig. 18), by removing soot from the flame nozzle (fig. 19) or by replacing a worn or damaged nozzle completely (fig. 20).

Know your system

Get to know your system before starting work on it. The illustration above depicts a British system; Australian and NZ systems are similar except for having direct water supplies. A variable-head pump drives water round the radiator and hot water circuits according to demand, with a motorized valve switching the flow between the two circuits. The boiler itself may have a balanced flue (main illustration) or a conventional one (inset).

FITTING DOOR LOCKS

The rules for securing your home against unwelcome intruders are quite simple. Make it difficult for the criminal to break in and he will go and look for easier pickings elsewhere

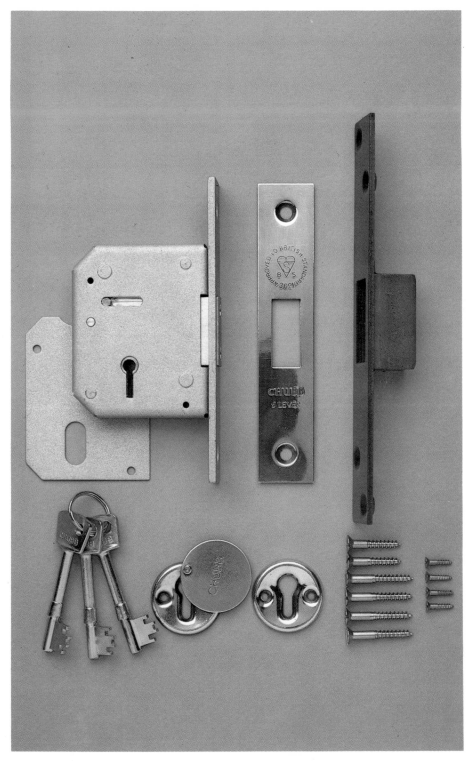

According to police, burglars fall into three basic categories. The professional thief who knows what he is after —valuables like antiques, jewellery, paintings and cash—likes to work quickly and cleanly.

The spur-of-the-moment sneak thief is the one who grabs at the chance of stealing ready cash and any easily transportable valuables if he sees a housewife pop next-door and leave the door open.

The third category is the young vandal, bent on causing as much damage as possible, who rips out telephone wires, slashes furniture and breaks everything he can lay his hands on.

Strong security locks on all your doors will help deter the last two categories. Professional burglars are more difficult to stop, but if your house is going to be very difficult to break into, they will usually decide to try elsewhere.

Securing doors

Most front doors are fitted with a nightlatch, which normally presents little trouble for a thief. A far more effective deterrent is a mortise deadlock. The bolt on this is fixed dead when locked and cannot be sprung back like an ordinary nightlatch.

Mortise locks come in a wide range of shapes and sizes but not all are of a guaranteed quality. It is best to buy locks which have been tested by an independent standards organization.

A good quality mortise lock is designed to be stronger than any wooden door into which it is likely to be fitted. This means that the woodwork would fail before the lock itself. When it is locked, the bolt is enclosed in a steel box protecting the head of the bolt against possible attack from a jemmy or similar tool.

Good security locks cannot be opened with skeleton keys and it is virtually impossible to pick them as they incorporate an anti-picking device. The deadbolts are reinforced to frustrate any attempt to cut right through the bolt.

Left: *All you need to make a door burglar-proof. A mortise lock provides an effective deterrent to most burglars, being difficult to force, or pick open. Fitting one is a fairly simple procedure—you will need a drill, chisel, padsaw and screwdriver*

1 Use the lock body as a template to mark the position of the hole in the edge of the door. Follow the same procedure on the sides

2 With a marking gauge set to half the thickness of the door, scribe a line down the door edge to mark the positions of the drill holes

3 The drill holes should run almost together along the centre line on the door edge. This leaves you with a minimum of chiselling work

4 Use the chisel carefully, paring away only a small amount of wood at a time. Open out the holes into a perfect rectangle

5 Having chiselled out the rebate for the facing plate around the hole, use the lock body again to help mark the position of the keyhole

6 Form the cut-out section of the keyhole with a padsaw. Check the key for fit from both sides before you install the lock body

Fitting a mortise lock

When you buy a mortise lock you are supplied with several parts that have to be assembled in a certain order. The parts include the main lock body —inset into the edge of the door— a plate that is screwed over this to hold it in place, a striking plate and box that fits into the outer frame, screws, keys, and the keyhole covers.

Marking the position

The mortise lock can be placed at any height on the door, though a central position will obviously give the strongest fastening. When you have decided where to place it, take the lock body and use it as a template to mark the width and depth on both sides of the door. Remember that the facing piece of the lock is sunk about 3 or 4mm into the door so that the cover plate is flush with the surface of the edge.

Use a try-square to mark the width of the lock body on the edge of the door. Then, with a marking gauge, score a line down this width—to fall exactly in the middle of the depth of the door (fig. 2).

To make the hole for the mortise lock, drill, then chisel flat, four holes in the edge of the door. For this,

you need a 19mm wood drill bit and a 19mm wood chisel. Wrap a short length of masking tape round the drill bit at the depth of the hole you require. When the holes are drilled, pare away the excess wood with the chisel, removing only small pieces at a time. Work progressively through the hole, making sure that the back surface is absolutely flat to avoid fitting problems later (figs. 3 and 4).

Chiselling out the rebate

Your next job is to chisel out the area into which the facing piece of the lock is inserted. A quick and easy way of doing this is to hold the cover plate in place and score carefully round it with a handyman's knife.

Remove the plate then carefully chisel out the area within the lines you have cut. You will probably find that you can score deeply enough with the knife to attain the recess depth that you require. The neatness and accuracy of this chiselling is a matter of coordinating hand and eye, but be careful not to cut too vigorously or you may go too deep. When you have finished try the lock body and the cover plate in position and make sure the plate lies flush.

Cutting the key-holes

Hold the lock body in position against the lines you have marked on the side of the door then mark a central point for the key-hole by placing a scriber or small drill bit through it (fig. 5). Repeat this operation on the other side. You then require a 12mm drill bit to bore two holes through to the centre from either side of the door. You will be able to determine, with your particular key, the length of the downward cut that you need to make for the key shape. Cut out this shape with a padsaw (fig. 6). Again make sure that you do this on both sides.

Now you can place the mortise lock back into position and screw on the cover plate. Your last task on this part of the door is to fix the key-hole covers on to the holes you have cut in the sides. You are provided with two covers, one with swivelling plate attached and one without. The swivel attachment is for the prevention of draughts and is therefore fixed on the inside of the door.

Mark the screw holes for these covers with the key comfortably set in the turning position. If you do not do it this way you may find you have key-fitting problems after the cover has been screwed in place.

7 *Having located the lock body in position and made any necessary adjustments to the depth of the rebate, screw on the cover plate*

8 *The only work left on the door itself is to fix the keyhole covers. Make sure the one with the draught cover goes on the inside*

9 *With the lock closed and held against the door frame, you can mark the depth of the striking plate rebate and bolt box*

10 *Cut out the hole for the bolt box and striking plate in the frame. Before securing the plate, make sure that the door will close properly*

11 *Both sides of the finished lock. The design is such that the woodwork around the door will fail before the lock itself*

12 *Provide additional protection for your front door by installing a pair of hinge bolts. These fit into recesses in the frame*

13 *A door security chain or bar allows you to open the front door slightly to unknown callers. Fixings must be strong*

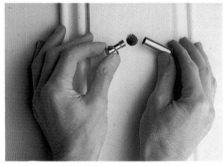

14 *If you have a solid front door, fit a viewer so you can check on callers. Drill a hole through the door and screw the parts together*

Fitting the striking plate

All that now remains is to fit the striking plate and bolt box onto the door frame.

To mark the position of the rebate, turn the key in the mortise lock so that the bolt protrudes in its locked position. Then close the door and, using the bolt as a guide, draw lines either side of it on the side of the door frame. Remember that the box that houses the bolt is wider than the bolt itself, so allow at least 3mm on either side of the bolt's width when you run these lines on to the inside of the door frame.

Next you must measure the length from the edge to the centre of the bolt on the lock body and translate this length on to the door frame, again using a marking gauge to scribe a central line on the wood.

It now remains to drill, as before, the box hole with two consecutively-placed holes (or three at the most) using the 19mm drill bit. This done, chisel and pare away the excess wood until the finished hole is formed.

It may not be necessary to make the striking plate flush with the level of the door frame's surface—it depends on how tightly the door fits in the

frame. If it is a very close fit you must repeat the operation of holding the plate into position, scoring round it and chiselling out a recess. If there is a gap where the door meets the frame, simply screw the striking plate into position. If, however, the screw holes on the striking plate are *plunged* —punched into a slight bowl-shaped recess—you may have to countersink the holes in the door frame slightly to allow for this.

Additional security

A good lock goes a long way to making a door secure. You can provide additional protection to the hinge edge of the door by fitting a pair of hinge bolts (fig. 12), one just below the top hinge and the other above the bottom one. Start by marking and drilling a hole in the door edge; then hammer in the reinforced bolt, and close the door so the protruding bolt marks the frame. Drill another hole at this point and fit a striking plate over it. Check that the bolts sit neatly in the holes as the door is closed.

To protect yourself from unwelcome callers, fit a door security chain (fig. 13) or a door viewer (fig. 14). Make sure that the screws securing the chain and its keeper are strong enough to prevent forcing by a would-be intruder. Viewers come in two halves which are screwed together.

Vulnerable points around your home

Right: *Erect high walls or fences to deter intruders (1). Fit gates with bolts or a padlock (2). If you have to leave ladders out of doors, padlock them to stout wall brackets (3). Always lock garage doors, (4). Coat metal downpipes leading to flat roofs or upstairs windows with anti-climb paint (5). Never leave upstairs windows open (6). Make sure all doors are fitted with locks (7). Avoid strong trelliswork which a burglar could climb (8).*

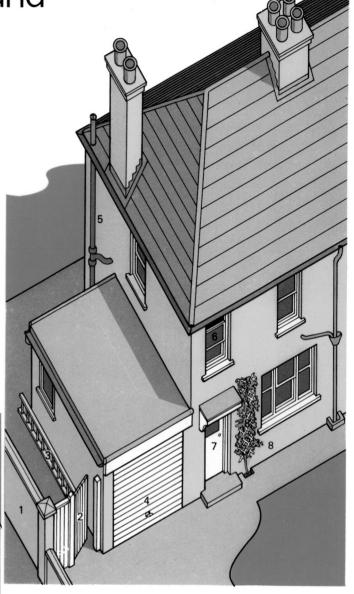

Left: *Light shady corners where a burglar could lurk (9). Keep ground floor windows closed whenever you're out, and fit window locks where possible (10). Don't leave fanlights open. Avoid fitting extractor fans in opening casements (11). Padlock sheds and other outbuildings (12). Secure back doors with bolts on the inside, plus a mortise deadlock (13). Fit special locks and anti-lift devices to patio doors (14). Lock or bolt skylights (15).*

FIXING FLOOR BOARDS

Floorboard repairs are straightforward and require few special tools. But repairs are essential for safety and for preserving the good condition of the joists beneath, and the floor covering above the boards

Above: *Use a strip of wood to protect the surface of the floorboards when prising out old nails*

Although solid and hardwearing, floorboard timbers are prone to all sorts of minor faults and irritations. For instance, creaks under the carpet are annoying but not dangerous; rotten boards which collapse underfoot can be dangerous as well as annoying. Even if your floorboarding is in perfect condition, it may still need work to improve draughtproofing—or to get to wiring underneath.

Types of floorboard
Most floorboards are made of softwood—usually pine. In a single-skin floor as used in Britain, the boards are fixed at right angles to the joists which support them, and may be nailed or screwed in

place. The board ends are arranged to concide with the joists, so that the join lies over the centre of the joist, for maximum support. In a double-skin floor as used in North America, the sub-floor is usually of plywood or wafer board, but the main floorboards are still at right angles to the joists.

Floorboards fall into two basic types: square-edged, and tongue-and-grooved (fig. D). Tongued-and-grooved (T&G) boards and their derivatives are designed to eliminate draughty gaps but are more difficult to take up than their square-edged counterparts.

If you are in any doubt which of the two types is used for your flooring, choose two boards with a slight gap between them and slide a knife blade in

as far as possible—compacted grime or draughtproofing in the gap may have to be scratched out first. If the blade is stopped, the boards are either tongued or rebated.

Lifting square-edged boards
For your starting point, choose the most convenient free end of the board you wish to lift. If the board extends right across the room and under the skirting (baseboard) on both sides, you have to start lifting it in the middle and work gradually towards the ends. When all the nails are loose, you spring the board free by pulling it upwards into a bow shape.

To lift the board, insert a bolster into the joint gap between it and the board

Joists and floorboards

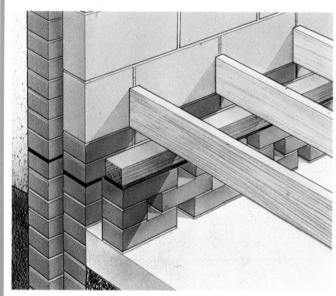

A. *Joists of a suspended floor are supported on small sleeper walls or piers on a concrete base*

B. *Metal joist hangers built into the inner wall are one method of supporting an upstairs floor*

C. *Flooring joists can also be built into the inner of two masonry walls*

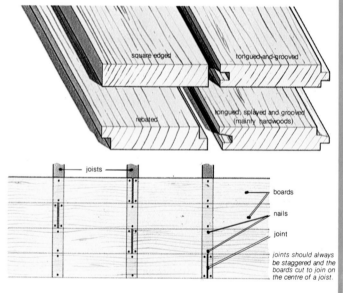

D. *Types of floorboard. Square-edged boards are found in older British houses, tongued boards elsewhere*

on one side, in line with the nails at the free end. Use a club hammer to drive it home. Then stamp on the bolster to push it down towards the floor (fig E). Do the same on the other side of the board.

As the board is levered up, insert the claw of a hammer under the end and continue levering up from here until the board comes completely free of the joist.

To help lift the rest of the board, insert a metal bar, length of stout timber or piping underneath the free end. Use the bolster and hammer to loosen the board at each line of nails, then lever it clear with the metal bar. For safety, immediately remove any exposed nails—particularly those left upright in the joists. A crowbar is much easier than a claw hammer for this job.

If a board proves particularly stub-

born, try to free one end and insert a metal bar under it. Using the bar as a levering support, stamp on the free end. After each stamp there should be some 'give', so move the support along the board towards the next joist until the nails give way here.

Lifting T&G board
Start by choosing a suitable free end and section of board, well clear of the

skirting. To break the tongue, insert a bolster into the join between two adjacent boards at the end of the board you wish to lift (fig. E). Give the bolster a few sharp taps with a hammer, until you feel or hear the tongue below start to split. Continue until the split extends at least 75mm from the nails, or until you otherwise judge it to be clear of the joist. You can then replace the bolster with a saw, knowing that its blade will escape damage from floorboard nails.

You can use almost any type of saw but a compromise between the awkward length of a panel saw and the short length of usable blade on a tenon saw is a purpose-made *flooring saw* (fig. E).

If a power saw is used, set the sawing blade depth to about the thickness of the board to avoid any damage to the sub-floor (if any), or to pipes or wires suspended below the flooring.

Continue cutting between the two boards until you are about 75mm from the next line of nails, and once again use the bolster to break the tongue along the stretch over the joists.

When the tongue is fully severed, use the bolster, claw hammer and

metal bar to lever up the board as you would do to lift a square-edged one. In this case, though, concentrate your levering activities at the end and along the severed side of the board at each joist. You should be able to lift the nails and tilt the board enough for the interlocked side to slide free of the adjacent board.

Well-fitted tongued-and-grooved boards may be so tightly cramped together that splitting them apart with a bolster and hammer may not be possible without causing extensive damage to both boards. In this case, the board you wish to remove must be split lengthways at the middle. A power saw is best for this job.

Cutting across floorboards

In a single-skin floor of the sort used in Britain, it is best to cut across a floorboard either over a joist or to the side of one, so that support for the new board ends is readily available. Cutting over a joist is a little more difficult than cutting beside one, but enables you to nail the cut section straight back in place. A double-skin floor can be cut anywhere, but try to avoid having two cut ends side-by-side on the floor.

1 To remove a damaged section, first locate a joist position. Mark a cutting line either over the middle of the joist or to one side of it

Cutting on a joist: It is important to make the cut along the centre of the joist, otherwise one or other of the two freshly-made board ends is not going to be supported properly.

The centre line of the joist can be pin-pointed by following on the line of nails of adjacent boards and board ends. Use a try square to pencil a cutting mark on a line joining the farthest possible reference points on each side of the board you are cutting. You can do this by eye or, better, by stretching a piece of string over the distance between the two points. If you are cutting alongside a board with a clearly indicated joist, just continue the line of the board end (or fixings) when marking the cutting line. If the nails are staggered, take a common centre-line from as many boards as possible.

To make the cut, you can leave the board in place and use a padsaw, compass saw or power jig saw. But if the board is long enough, it is easier to lift it up into a 'hump' and cut with a tenon saw or flooring saw. To do this, you lever the board upwards with the bolster and then support it with two offcuts of timber wedged beneath it.

Cutting beside a joist: First locate the side of the joist. You may be able to do this by inserting a knife or metal rule into the gap between the floorboards, sliding it along until it hits the joist. Mark the board at this point, and use a try square to complete the cutting line. Alternatively, and if there is a gap between the floorboards on the other side, repeat probing and simply join up the two points marked on the board (fig. 1).

Drill an 8mm hole up against and at

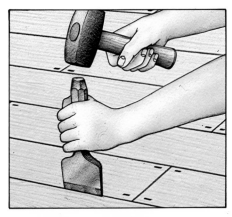

E. A bolster (top pictures) is used both to break the tongues of T&G boards and to loosen the edges of boards. A claw hammer is useful for lifting boards, and a flooring saw for cutting out shorter lengths

2 Using a piece of wood as a guide, scratch and then tease a cut with the first few teeth if you are using a tenon saw to cut on the joist

3 If you are using a padsaw or power jig saw to make a cut beside a joist, drill a small hole the width of the blade

4 Use a padsaw or compass saw to cut right across the board or, if you prefer, just to give you a slot in which to start off your handsaw

5 A padsaw can be used to sever the tongue of a tongued-and-grooved board if other forms of sawing are impracticable

6 Remove nails from the joist using a claw hammer. Protect the board alongside with an offcut. Do not hammer old nails into the joists

7 When making an extra support, start by cutting a generous length of stout timber. The extra width ensures that the board is firmly fixed

8 Mark the floorboard gap on the upper surface of the bearer. As you can see the bearer straddles the gap and acts just like the joist

9 Partly face-nail the support, to the point when the nails are just about to break through on the other side of the timber

10 Complete the nailing while pushing the bearer against the joist and upwards against the fixed boards on both sides

one end of the cutting line (fig. 3) then use a padsaw or power jig saw to cut next to, and along, the cutting line. The padsaw can be replaced with a handsaw or circular-blade power saw when convenient, and re-used if necessary at the end of the cut.

Fitting an extra bearer

If you have removed a section of floorboard by cutting along the side of a joist, you must fit an extra bit of timber to the joist, in order to provide support for the new board end.

Make this bearer from an offcut of softwood, whose minimum dimensions ought to be no less than 38mm by 50mm. Cut it to length, slightly longer than the width of floorboarding removed and use either nails or screws for fixing it in place (fig. 9). If you choose nails, use two or three about 75mm long for each floorboard width, and hammer these partially into the broader side before positioning the bearer. If you use screws, two for each board width are enough, but drill pilot holes before fitting them.

Position the bearer against the joist and make sure that the top edges of both pieces of timber are exactly flush. Pull the bearer upwards, tightly against the floorboards on either side, while you hammer or screw it securely in place (fig. 10).

Replacing square-edged boards

There are few problems in replacing square-edged boards. New ones of the same thickness are cut to length and—in the case of non-standard sizes—to width. If part of the board has to be tapered or otherwise shaped to fit, use the discarded board as a template when

you saw to shape the new one.

If a single board is to be replaced simply slot it into place and nail down. A number of boards covering a large area are best fitted individually—if possible in the same flooring 'pattern' as originally. No two board ends should lie side by side on the same joist.

When fitting a number of boards, do a 'dry run' first to check the width fit, and whether tight butting of the boards is possible. Where the boards are to remain visible, keep to the original spacings for the sake of appearance.

If a complete floor area is being replaced, make a point of butting all boards as tightly as possible before fixing. This is done with a floor cramp —available from hire shops—and substantially improves underfloor draught-proofing (fig. 18).

11 *If fitting a thicker board than the rest, a cut-out has to be made where the board crosses a joist. First mark the joist's position*

13 *Carefully cut the board in order not to exceed the required rebate depth—this can be gauged by sight or by direct measurement*

If part of the original floorboarding is to be replaced, cut off any wood which is badly split where nails were removed. Do not re-use old nail holes. These, and new holes along the length of the board, should be made good with a filler paste.

Replacing T&G boards

Replacing tongued-and-grooved boards is not quite so straightforward. If you are re-using the old board, this can be replaced by fitting the remaining tongued or grooved side into the adjacent board. A small gap will remain on the other side—this must be plugged for complete draught-proofing.

To fit a new tongued and grooved board, you may have to plane off its tongue to get it to fit, but leave its grooved side intact.

12 *Transfer the marks from the underside of the replacement floorboard to its edges. Repeat this step at every joist position*

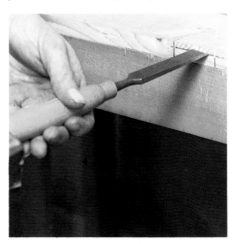

14 *Use a chisel to remove wood between the cutting lines. The chisel face should be down. Work in stages to end with a level cut*

15 *Check that the rebate fits snugly and is of the required depth. Continue chiselling if the board is proud of those alongside*

If a number of adjacent boards have been removed, any necessary combination of used and new boards may be used when reflooring. The technique is to loosely fit these together over the floor area to be covered, in the process forming a low arch by making the boards slightly over-sized. Lay a spare plank over this, and press or stamp the boards down: the tongues and grooves knit together in the process. The flattened boards can then be fixed in place. Alternatively, you can use an off-cut and mallet as in fig. 17.

Replacing short sections

If you are cutting out and replacing a short section of floorboard you may want to use up a spare piece of timber lying about the house. Alternatively, you may have difficulty getting a re-placement board which exactly matches the thickness of your existing ones. Either way, the new board will be better too thick than too thin.

Having cut your new section to length, lay it beside the gap in the floor and mark off on the underside where it is to pass over a joist. Chisel out rough rebates between the marks, to the same depth as the board is oversize (fig. 14).

When you lay the board, the rebates should fit over the joists and allow it to rest flush with the others.

Dealing with creaking boards

Loose and creaking floorboards may be caused by incorrect nailing, by the joists below them settling, or by warping and shrinkage. It is usually possible to cure a loose board simply by re-nailing or screwing it back in place.

But before you do this, check that the loose joint coincides with the centre of the joist below, taking the board up if necessary. If it does not, widen the joist with a new bearer (figs. 7-10), or replace the whole board.

To nail floorboards, use 50mm lost-head nails or flooring nails. Position them next to, and about 12mm away from, the existing nails. When you have finished, drive all the nail heads well below the surface of the board with a nail punch (nail set).

To secure floorboards with screws, use 40mm countersunk steel screws. Drill pilot holes for them 12mm from each existing nail, taking care that the holes go no deeper than the thickness of the board. When all the screws are in place, make sure that none of them protrudes above the surface.

16 *If the replacement board is too thin, use sheet wood to make up the difference. Do not use newspaper folds for this job*

17 *When replacing tongued boards the last two will need force before slipping into fit—use a mallet and protective wood offcut*

18 *Nailing boards into place. A pencil line ensures accuracy. A floor cramp—worth hiring for big jobs—keeps the boards tightly packed*

19 *If you decide to use nails for fixing a floorboard in place, hammer in the heads using a punch. Use filler and stain to conceal the hole*

20 *If you choose to screw down a board, drill a hole to accept the screw body only. This minimizes the effort needed in fixing boards*

21 *Use a countersink bit to drill a recess for the screw head and— if necessary—fill the hole once the board has been screwed to the joist*

REPAIRING SKIRTING

The purpose of skirting boards is twofold. They serve as a protective buffer at the base of walls, preserving the wall finish from abrasion, and they also act as a decorative feature

Skirting boards can be fixed to a wall in several different ways. In timber-frame construction, they are simply nailed directly through the plasterboard and into the studs, or vertical timbers, behind.

In masonry walls, nails can be hammered at an angle through the board and its backing of plaster into the brickwork (fig. A). Alternatively, strips of wood called grounds can be used. These are firmly attached to the wall and act as a fixing base for skirting boards placed over them. A continuous strip is supported at intervals by small upright pieces called soldiers (fig. B).

With either system, some plaster damage must be expected as the old skirtings are removed, and usually needs to be made good with plaster or filler before new boards are fixed.

In rare instances, the skirting is fixed to wedge-shaped uprights bedded into cavities in the brickwork (fig. C). Installed at the time the wall was made, these are held in place by a

mortar filling which often decays over a period of time. Excessive force on the skirting—such as that required to remove it—is often sufficient to dislodge these uprights. If this happens, mortar them back in. A new upright can be made by tapering a suitable length of batten.

The golden rule to bear in mind when dealing with skirting board is to be careful. The bedding plaster is easily chipped by a casual knock.

Removing and replacing boards

To remove a length of skirting, start at one of the corners and place a bolster on the top edge where the skirting meets the wall. Using a claw hammer, hammer the bolster gently down. This will prise the skirting away from the wall at that point. Continue this action along the length

of skirting to be removed. Where greater resistance is met, the skirting will have been nailed to the wall.

With the top edge prised away from the wall you can start to remove the skirting completely. For this you need a claw hammer and a small, thin piece of plywood or hardboard to protect the wall finish. Place the claw of the hammer down behind the top edge of the board and slip the timber between the claw and the wall. Lever gently upwards on the handle, pressing the hammer head against the timber. This forces the board further away from the wall and draws out the nails at the same time.

Always use timber or a piece of hardboard to protect the wall or the hammer may leave an indent. Do not use a crowbar as this can damage the wall plaster.

Once the skirting is removed the nails should be pulled out. Use a pair of pincers to draw out the nails from the back of the board. This keeps the paint surface intact, as the face of the board often splinters if the nails are hammered through and drawn out from the front.

Partial removal of skirting

When the area of damaged or decayed skirting is relatively small, partial replacement is more economical. Measure the length of board to be replaced and buy or make a new piece to match.

First, prise the damaged part of the board away from the wall with a bolster (fig. 1). With the top edge free, you can now insert a timber wedge between the board and the wall at the place where the first cut is to be made. The wedge should have one sloping face and be thick enough to push the board out by about 40mm. Position the wedge with the flat face to the wall so that as you hammer it down, the sloping face pushes the skirting away from the wall.

To cut out the damaged length of board, make a mitred cut at each end using a mitre block or box. There are no set rules for positioning the direction of the mitres: they can be parallel or face in opposite directions, and lean inwards or outwards.

Position the mitre block with its back against the face of the skirting and the top level with, or above the top of the skirting. If necessary, put

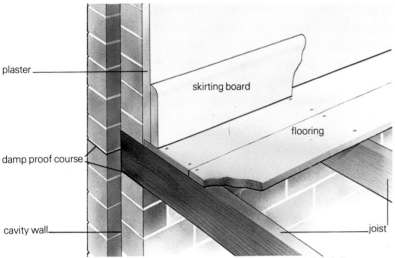

A. *Skirting fixed directly to the masonry. On a plastered brick wall, plaster damage usually accompanies the skirting board's removal, especially if the nails securing the board have rusted*

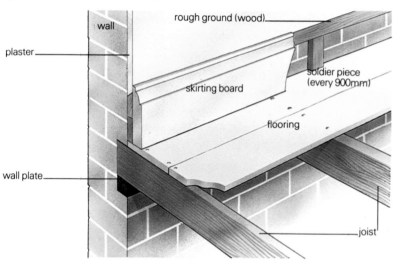

B. *Skirting fixed to a rough ground supported clear of the floor. Board removal may cause partial collapse of the ground and plaster base it supports*

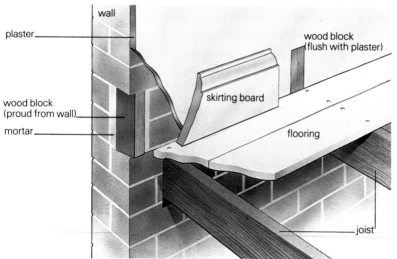

C. *Skirting fixed to wood blocks set in the wall at the time of building. Retaining mortar may have decayed, and both this and damp soldiers have to be made good before replacing skirting*

some suitable packing material under the block to raise it to this level. Make the first cut at the end of the damaged area using a panel saw in short rapid strokes (fig. 6). Only the first few teeth of the saw are used so these teeth must be sharp.

Continue the rapid strokes until the teeth of the saw reach the base of the block. Remove the block in order to complete the cutting down to the floor, taking great care to maintain the straight line of the cut. Pull out the wedge and reposition it where the second cut is to be made at the other end of the damaged piece of skirting. The second cut is made in the same way. Once free, lift out the piece of board from the skirting.

Fitting the replacement board
Using the mitre block, cut a mitre at one end of the new board. Make sure that the direction of the cut is the same as that of the first cut, made when removing the damaged piece. After cutting the mitre, measure the inside edge of the area to be fitted with new skirting and transfer the measurement to the replacement board. Use the mitre block again to cut the second mitre. Check that the direction of the cut matches that in the skirting. Fit the replacement piece in the gap to check its compatability. If adjustment is necessary, use a plane with the blade set finely and remove a few shavings from the end grain.

Fixing the replacement board
An easy method of fixing the new length of board is to use 38mm oval pins and skew nail them through the mitre joints. This way, you will nail through both thicknesses of skirting. Punch the nail heads below the surface and make good the indentations with a little woodworking filler.

Alternatively, you can use masonry nails to fix the skirting into the brickwork behind. In this case, a piece of timber the same thickness as the plaster should be placed behind to overlap the old and new pieces of skirting at each end. This ensures that the skirting will not be pushed out of its vertical position should it be knocked at the bottom.

Matching new skirting to old
New houses usually have one of the following types of skirting: pencil round, splayed, splayed-and-rounded, or chamfered. These are easier to obtain than the elaborate older boards but fill-in pieces can be made from a square-edged board.

1 Place a bolster behind the top edge of the skirting board. Hammer the bolster down gently. Repeat along the length of skirting

2 Place the claw of the hammer behind the skirting and slip the protective board between it and the wall. Lever the board away

3 If a board proves particularly stubborn, hammer a row of wedges down behind it. This reduces the risk of splitting the board

4 When the whole length of skirting has been levered from the wall, draw out the nails from the board using a pair of pincers

5 If a damaged length is to be removed, first drive in a wedge, then place a mitre block against the skirting while you start your cut

6 Now continue the cut to the bottom of the board, having first ruled a vertical pencil line to help keep the cut straight

7 You may have to match new board to old skirting. For a 'pencil round', mark a line 6mm from the front top edge and plane it round

8 For splayed skirting, mark the desired thickness on the top of the board and the end of the incline on the face. Then plane down

9 For splayed and rounded skirting, mark off the top of the board as for a pencil round and plane and sand the edge

10 For an angled board, mark the correct thickness on the top of the board and the angle required on both the end grains. Plane down

11 A variety of skirting styles can be manufactured from ordinary board or from a combination of board and moulding

12 To join a new section part-way along a wall, first measure the length you need and mark it on the back of the replacement board

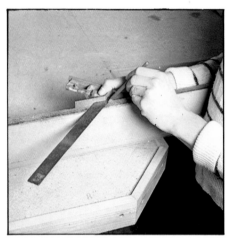

13 Next, mark a mitre across the top of the board, joining this mark to the one on the back. Make sure the mitre slopes the right way

14 Cut through the board to form the mitre—either 'free-hand', as here, or using a mitre box or mitre block. A true cut is essential

15 Position the board to check for fit, remembering to remove bits of plaster or other obstructions. If necessary, trim it with the plane

16 Nail the board into place once a fitting check has been made. Use suitable filler to conceal the nail holes you have drilled

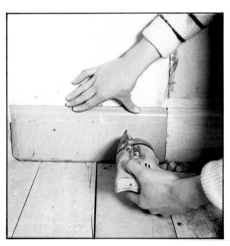

17 Another technique of fitting boards is to drill a well for the nail head and then fill this with filler after the nail has been hammered in

18 The completed section should join inconspicuously with existing skirting if the job of matching and fitting has been properly done

Dealing with corners

For pencil round skirting, for example, mark a line along the face of a square-edge board, about 6mm down from what will in effect be the top leading edge. Carefully round this edge as you plane down to the 6mm mark. It helps to start with the plane level, at the top, curving round the edge as you plane down the edge along its length.

Splayed skirting—where the face of the board is sloped slightly upwards—is almost as straightforward. Mark the desired thickness at the top, and where you want the face to end. Then plane down between these two lines.

Skirting a room

Skirting a whole room is in many ways much easier than repairing existing skirtings. You do not have the problem of matching new skirting to old and, as skirting can be purchased in full lengths to suit room walls, you will have no joints to make in the length of the boards.

The one rule when skirting a room is that external corners have a mitred joint and internal corners have a scribed one. Apart from that, it is sensible to work round the room in rotation. Doing this gives you a scribed cut at one end of a board. The other end will be either square cut (for another scribed joint) or mitred, depending on whether the board meets another internal or external corner.

When using masonry nails always wear plastic goggles as the nails are brittle and may break if they are not struck squarely.

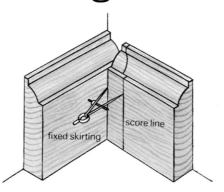

D. *Dividers can scribe complex shapes of moulding to a new board*

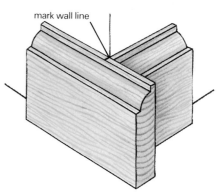

E. *Scribing the mitre joint when finishing an external corner*

External corners

Mitred joints pose no problem if made carefully with a cutting guide such as a mitre block. However, once placed against the wall, the inevitable irregularities in the plaster may cause a few small gaps to develop. Fill these with filler paste: when dry and decorated they will not show.

If you can, make these mitred cuts with a mitre box and panel saw. If not, use a jig saw. First, mark a piece of board to length and cut it 50mm oversize (fig. E). Hold it in place against the wall and carefully mark the inner measurement of the mitre joint. To do this, hold a try square at right angles to the board and close against the other wall. Add the width of the board to this measurement and mark off, continuing the line down the face of the board.

Set the sole plate on the jig saw to an angle of 45 degrees. Instructions for this accompany the different makes of saw. Cramp the board firmly—face upwards—and set the jig saw blade against the pencil line. Mark on the board the right-hand edge of the jig saw sole plate and extend this line across the board. Measure the gap between the lines at both ends to check that the line is straight. Take a small timber offcut and put it on this line, holding it firmly in place with a cramp. This provides a straight and secure edge against which to press the sole plate. Saw across the board keeping the plate pressed closely against the offcut and the result will be a perfectly cut mitre. Use glasspaper to smooth off any rough fibres left after the cut has been made.

Cut a second mitre on the adjoining length of board, using the jigsaw in exactly the same way. Check before making the cut that the mitre is running in the right direction.

19 *For an external corner, hold the board against the wall and mark in pencil the end of the wall with a straightedge (see also fig. E)*

20 *Add to this the thickness of the board. Draw a line across the face. Set the jigsaw blade to the width of the sole plate*

Now position the first length of board against the wall and measure from the tip of the mitre to the wall to determine the exact length. Transfer this measurement to the board and cut a square edge for the butt joint with a panel saw.

Before nailing the skirting to the wall, a replacement ground must be fitted if the old one is no longer intact or has rotted. Use masonry nails to fix the grounds into the brickwork, below the plaster (see fig. B). Mark the position of the soldiers on the floorboard below, so that you know where to nail when the skirting board has covered them. Use nails to fix the skirting to the ground support and punch the heads below the surface so that they can be filled over. It's a good idea to treat grounds and soldiers with wood preservative first.

Internal corners

A scribed joint is used on internal angles. You cut one board to length with a square end, then cut the second to a shape that fits against the curved or moulded end of the first board. This joint is used because, unlike a mitre, it cannot open up—leaving a gap between the boards—as you nail the skirtings to the walls.

There are two ways of obtaining the scribed shape on the second board. One is to use a pair of dividers to trace the profile of one board onto the other. Then you cut out this profile with a coping saw, keyhole saw or jigsaw.

A better way is to start by fixing the first board (the square-ended one) in place. Then, on the second board, you cut a mitre. This leaves a profiled outline on the surface of the board. So you cramp the board firmly and cut around this outline—at right angles to the board's surface—with your coping saw, keyhole saw or jigsaw. The process is easier to do than to describe or illustrate, but if you practise on an offcut first you will soon get the hang of it.

However you fix the skirting to the wall or ground, make sure the board is firmly in place—particularly where knocks are common, such as near doorways, sockets and external corners that are always in an exposed position. A firm fixing can prevent considerable additional damage to plaster and grounds that ought really to have been replaced long before they work loose.

If you are left with gaps between the skirting and the floor surface, pin lengths of slim quadrant bead to the bottom face of the boards.

21 *Cramp an offcut to this mark and set the saw blade to 45°. Saw along the pencil line pressing the sole plate firmly against the offcut*

22 *Fix this board to the wall with masonry nails. Take care when hammering to avoid brickwork or plaster damage beneath*

23 *Cut a mitre on a second length of board. Measure off and cut to length, leaving a square end to go into the inside corner*

24 *Using a keyhole saw, cut along the outline on the face of the board which has been displayed by cutting the mitre first*

25 *Join the two boards with two or three nails, nailing through one mitred edge into the other. Punch the nail heads down*

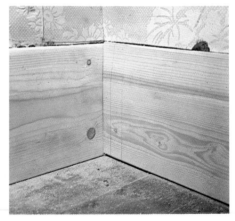

26 *Measure and cut the board to length to fit over the square end of the previous length of board. To get a perfect fit, tap it down*

REPAIRING WINDOW FRAMES

It is essential to keep timber-framed windows in prime condition—if neglected, the wood will quickly deteriorate. And if signs of decay are left uncorrected, rot may set in

Below: *Sash cords are fitted into grooves in the side of the sash and held in place by four or five clout nails. Sash cords inevitably fray through constant use and age and eventually need replacing*

A neglected window spoils the appearance of a home, causes draughts and damp, and can tempt intruders. If the signs of decay are not detected and dealt with at an early stage, further deterioration will make repair more difficult.

Types of window
The two basic types of timber-framed window are the casement sash (fig. C) and the double-hung sliding sash window (fig. B).

The sliding sash window operates by means of cords, pulleys and weights which counterbalance the sashes—the opening parts of the window—as they slide up and down. Two sets of beadings —thin lengths of wood—hold the

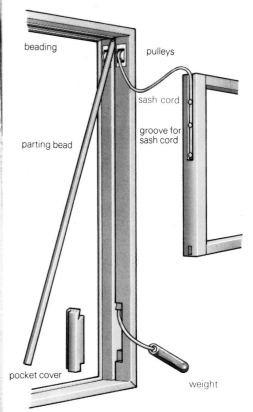

beading

pulleys

sash cord

groove for sash cord

parting bead

pocket cover

weight

A. *Components of a sash window. The sash cord is nailed to the edge of the sash and tied to a weight*

sashes straight in the frame. Covers or caps in the lower part of the inner edge of the frame are usually provided to allow access to the compartments containing the weights. Where this is not so you will have to remove the inside frame cover. Modern sash windows usually have spring-operated mechanisms instead of cords, and these are simply replaced if they fail.

A casement window is attached to the frame by hinges and is held open by means of a stay which is designed to allow progressive adjustment. It is the most common style of window.

Working considerations

The most common problems affecting timber-framed windows are decay from wet rot, loose joints in the sashes and —in the case of sash windows—fraying or broken sash cords. To repair these faults you have to remove the sash so that you can get at the individual components of the window or work on the sash itself—difficult or impossible if it were left standing in the frame.

Where a section of a sash is decayed, you can strengthen it by cutting out

and renewing the affected part of the wood. If the joints which hold the sash together are working loose, you can reinforce these by knocking them apart and re-assembling them with fresh adhesive. But if the decay is particularly widespread, rot may have irreparably damaged the whole sash and the only solution is to discard it and fit a new one.

If you have modern casement windows, replacing a decayed section of the casement may be difficult because there is insufficient wood to work with. In this case, it may be quicker and probably more effective to replace the faulty casement altogether.

If you are dealing with a window affected by rot, it is best to carry out the work during dry weather as the timber remains swollen in damp conditions, making any repairs less than perfect after eventual shrinkage in dry, warm conditions.

Before starting work, identify the type of rot. Wet rot is more common in window frames but you may find dry rot in which case treatment must be more drastic.

Removing a casement window

Older types of casement windows are constructed from thick timber and are therefore heavy. So, if you have to remove the casement for replacement or repair, the work must be tackled with great care.

Begin by passing a strong cord around the window, under the top hinge, and tie this to the upper part of a step ladder to prevent the casement from falling to the ground.

Before you attempt to remove the screws holding the hinges in place, use an old paintbrush to dab a small amount of proprietary paint stripper on any paint around the screw heads.

If the screws prove particularly obstinate and difficult to turn, try to tighten them slightly first to help loosen the threads, or give the end of the screwdriver a few sharp taps with a mallet. If all else fails, try heating the head of the screw with a soldering iron to loosen the thread's grip.

Remove the screws which fix the hinges to the frame first—those in the casement are easier and safer to remove once you have taken the window

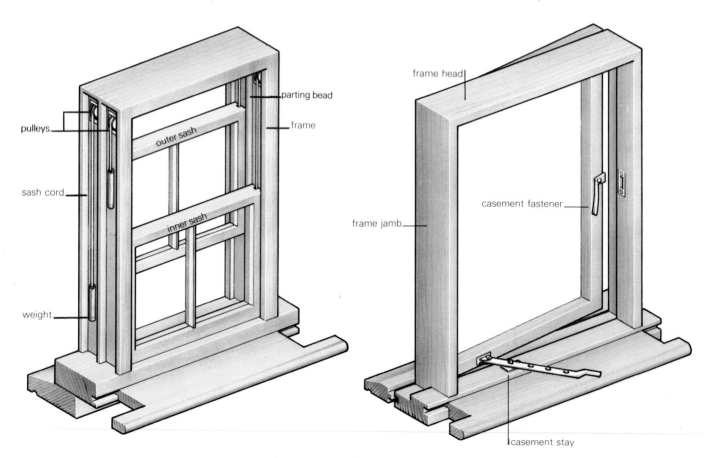

B. *The weights counterbalance the sashes, allowing them to slide up and down. The sashes are held in place by lengths of beading pinned into grooves*

C. *A casement window. The casement is attached to the frame by hinges. A casement stay holds it open and a fastener allows it to be shut tight*

1 To replace a sash cord, take the sash and parting bead from the frame, then remove the pocket cover to gain access to the weight compartment

2 Lay the cover aside, then remove the weight from the compartment and pull the old, decayed sash cord away from the frame

3 Tie some string to a small weight such as a nail, then thread this over the pulley wheel and out through the pocket opening

4 Tie the new cord to the string, pull this down through the pocket, then tie the end of the cord securely to the original weight

5 Pull the free end of the cord so that the weight is raised—25mm for the outer sash or almost to the pulley for the inner one

6 To hold the weight temporarily in position, half-drive a nail through the cord, securing it to the edge of the frame

7 Fit the new sash cord into the groove in the edge of the sash and fix it into place with four or five clout nails

out of the frame. Loosen each of the screws by one full turn and then unscrew two from each hinge, leaving one screw in each.

Now, starting with the upper hinge, remove the remaining screws. Give the casement extra support with one hand under the outer corner and then swing it sideways into the room or, if you are working on the ground floor, lower it to the ground.

Removing a sash window

If a sash window is neglected, it becomes difficult to open and close properly and eventually its cords may fray and snap. To cure these problems, it is usually necessary to remove both sashes from the frame.

Start by removing the fixing beads around the inside edge of the frame. Beginning with a long piece, use an old chisel to prise it away starting from the middle of its length. Bring it out to a distance of about 25mm from the frame and then tap it smartly back into place. This should cause the bead's fixing pins to rise up through the surface so that you can remove them with a pair of pincers.

Repeat this procedure for the remaining pieces of beading, then take out the inner, or lower, sash and rest it temporarily on the window sill. Ease the parting bead which runs between the two sashes from its housings then slide out the outer sash.

Sashcords are usually nailed into grooves in the sides of the sashes. To detach the cords of the inner sash, make pencil marks on the front of each sash to show where the ends of the cords reach to, then make corresponding marks on the outer frame.

Afterwards, remove the clout nails which hold the cords in place and—unless you intend to replace the cords—immediately tap the uppermost nails into the edges of the frame to prevent the weights on the other end of the cords from falling down behind the stile boards (fig. 6).

With both cords removed from the inner sash, you can take it from the frame and repeat the procedure for the outer one.

Replacing sash cords

If the frame of a sash window needs attention, it is likely that the sash cords are also in a poor condition and need to be replaced. And if one of the cords has already snapped, it is possible that the others are frayed and about to break, so it is best to replace all four at the same time.

For renewing the cords, buy a slightly longer length of pre-stretched wax cord than you need to allow for waste. You will also need a lump of lead or a large nail to act as a weight for dropping the new cords down into the pockets.

Remove the sashes from the frame, as described above, and begin work on the cords of the outer sash. To get to the weights to which they are attached, unscrew the pocket covers—or lever them out if they are simply nailed or wedged into place—then pull the weights through the pocket openings and remove the cords.

Check the pulleys to make sure that they run smoothly and, if not, apply a little oil to the pivots. If the window is in particularly bad condition, the pulleys may have rusted and you will have to replace them altogether.

To fix the first new cord, tie your nail or lead weight to a piece of string about 1.5m long and feed it over the groove of the outer pulley wheel until it falls down behind the stile. Tie the new sash cord to the other end of the string and pull it over the pulley and out through the pocket opening. Now untie the string, secure the cord to the original weight and replace this inside its compartment.

Pull the weight up about 25mm and half drive a nail through the cord, into the edge of the frame to hold the weight temporarily in position. Cut the cord so that it is level with the pencil mark on the frame, made when you first removed the sashes.

Next position the outer sash so that you can fit the cord into its groove, align the end of the cord with the pencil mark on the front of the sash, then fix the cord in place with four or five clout nails. Repeat the procedure for

8 If the mortise and tenon joints of a sash become loose, remove the sash from the frame so that you can re-assemble the joints

10 Knock the loose mortise and tenon joints apart, making sure that you protect the frame with a piece of waste timber

the other cord, remove the temporary nails and lift the sash back into place within the frame.

The procedure for renewing the cords of the inner sash is almost the same but in this case pull the weights up further, almost to the pulley, before fixing the temporary nails (fig. 5).

Then replace the pocket covers, parting bead, the inner sash and then the outer beading. Grease the channels with a little candle wax to aid smooth running.

In some windows, the cord may be knotted into a hole in the side of the sash. The method of replacing is much the same, but tying the knot in exactly the right place might require some trial and error.

Strengthening a sash

If the mortise and tenon joints of a

9 With the glass removed from the sash frame. use a shave hook to scrape away all traces of putty from the timber

11 Clean all the old glue from the tenons with wire wool, then clean the area in and around the mortises with an old, blunt chisel

12 Having made sure that the pin and socket of each joint are clean and dry, coat the tenons with waterproof woodworking adhesive

13 *Slide the tenons into position, then glue replacement wedges and fit them into place. Drive them home until the joint is secure*

14 *When all the joints have been re-assembled, check that the sash is square, then cramp it using an improvized web cramp*

sash become loose, water will eventually penetrate the gaps causing decay in the sash and possibly the surrounding timber as well. Extensive and costly repairs could then be the result of an initially minor fault.

Do not be tempted to strengthen a loose-jointed sash simply by filling the gaps. To do the job properly, remove the sash from the frame and chip away the putty holding the glass in place. Remove the glazing pins and the glass, then use a shave hook to scrape away all the remaining putty from the edges of the timber (fig. 9).

Now knock the joints apart, using a mallet with a timber offcut to protect the sash, and clean all the old glue from the tenons with wire wool. The joints in sashes are usually reinforced with two small wedges in each mortise to ensure a firm fit. Remove these and clean the inside of the mortises with an old, blunt chisel.

Using the removed wedges as a guide, mark up and cut replacements slightly longer than the originals to allow for trimming. When you have cut all the replacement wedges, coat the tenons with a waterproof woodworking adhesive and slide them into position in the mortises (fig. 12).

Tap them home with a mallet, again protecting the timber with a piece of waste wood, then apply some glue to two of your new wedges. With the angled edge of each wedge facing inwards, tap them into place with the mallet then trim off the ends with a chisel.

Fit the remaining wedges, and check that the sash frame is square by measuring the diagonals—which should be equal. Then cramp the sash. Sash cramps consist of two adjustable stops on a long bar; they come in different lengths up to 3m long with extensions. One stop is adjusted by sliding it along the bar and securing it with a pin; the other tightens like a vice jaw. Because of their size, sash cramps are expensive to buy, but they can be obtained from hire shops: this is probably a better way to get hold of them, as you are unlikely to use them very often.

Ensure that the surface of the wood does not get scratched and damaged by the action of the cramp by placing newspaper or a small block of wood between the cramp jaws and the frame. Make sure the sash is exactly square to the workpiece or distortions may result. During cramping, the bar of the sash will tend to bow in towards the workpiece, so place small wedges underneath to keep it straight while the glue is drying. Once the glue has set, you can reglaze the window and rehang the sash.

Renewing decayed timber

If part of a sash is affected by wet rot, make a probe into the wood with a bradawl to check the extent of the damage. Providing the decayed section is small and is spread over no more than half the thickness of the rail, you can cut out the affected wood and replace it with new timber.

Knock apart the joints as described above to remove the rail which needs repair from the rest of the sash frame. Use a combination square to mark a 45° angle at each end of the decayed area (fig. 15). Then mark horizontal lines slightly below the depth of the decayed section. Make these lines on both sides of the rail.

Next, secure the timber in a vice and saw down the angled lines to the depth line with a tenon saw. Use a

keyhole saw or a jigsaw to cut along the depth line and, with the waste wood removed, smooth down the sawn edges with a bevel-edged chisel.

Use the cut piece of wood as a pattern to measure up the replacement timber, then mark the cutting lines with the combination square.

Angles of 45° are easiest cut using a mitre box to guide the saw blade, but if you do not have one, continue the cutting lines around all the faces of the timber, then secure it in a vice and cut the replacement section. Plane down the sawn edges of the new wood and check its fit in the sash rail. If it is slightly oversize on any of its faces, sand down the unevenness.

The replacement wood is fixed into place by two or three screws, countersunk below the surface. Drill holes in the new section for these, staggering them slightly, then apply some glue to the underside and angled faces and cramp the section into place. Extend the screw holes into the sash rail to a depth of at least 12mm, drive in the screws and sink their heads well below the surface of the wood.

When the glue has set, remove the cramp and plane down the surfaces of the new wood until it is flush with the surrounding timber. Then reassemble the sash as described above.

Sticking windows

Apart from the faults already described, casements and sashes can stick because of a build-up of old paint or because the timber in the frame swells slightly.

The former problem is easily solved by removing the offending frame, stripping off all the old paint and then repainting. But swelling is a problem which can come and go with the weather. On casement windows, where it occurs most often, swelling can usually be allowed for by adjusting the casement hinges—a far less drastic solution than planing off the excess.

Mark the swollen part of the casement and judge whether increasing or decreasing the depth of one of the hinge recesses will bring it away from the window frame.

To increase the depth, pare away 2mm or so of wood from the recess with a sharp chisel. Try the casement for fit again before you start to remove any more.

To decrease the depth, cut a shim of cardboard or thin hardboard to the shape of the recess and fix it in place with a dab of glue. Punch or drill screw holes through the shim then replace the casement. Do this with great care to ensure a proper fit.

15 To replace a small section of decayed timber, mark a 45° angle at each end of the area of rot using a combination square

16 Mark horizontal lines slightly below the depth of the decayed section, then use a tenon saw to cut down the angled lines

17 Take care not to extend the cuts beyond the depth line, then saw along the horizontal line with a pad-saw or a jigsaw

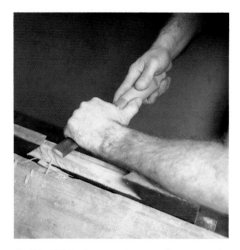

18 With the waste wood removed, use a bevel-edged chisel to smooth down the cut edges and sever any remaining fibres

19 Use the waste wood as a pattern to measure up replacement timber, then mark the cutting lines with the combination square

20 Cut out the replacement piece of timber, then drill holes for its fixing screws, down through the face of the new timber

21 Apply some glue to the new wood and lay it in place. Extend the screw holes into the sash rail, then drive the screws home

22 When the screws are in place and the glue set, plane down the faces of the new timber until it is flush with the surrounding wood

23 Now fill in the screw holes with wood filler, leave this to dry, then reglaze the sash and rehang it in the frame

STAIR PROBLEMS SOLVED

Timber staircases are complicated, intricate structures. But as they are also very strong, built to withstand years of use, they rarely give much trouble. And most minor faults that stairs are prone to are simple to deal with

Above: *The projecting front of a step is called a nosing. On an uncarpeted wooden staircase, nosings eventually become worn and therefore dangerous. Cut out a worn nosing and replace it with new wood cut to shape*

Wooden staircases are strong, long-lasting structures which seldom give much trouble beyond the occasional creaking step. But when the odd component in a stair does begin to deteriorate, it is best put right before accidents are allowed to happen.

Pages 65 and 66 show the most common types of timber staircase and their component parts. But as building methods vary widely from house to house, you may find that your stairs employ a mixture of the standard construction techniques illustrated.

Often, the most difficult aspect when dealing with stairs is getting access to the trouble spot. The underside of the stairs may be boarded over or covered with lath and plaster. And the space between the stairs and the floor is often partitioned in some way to provide an understairs cupboard.

Where access is a problem, you may have to choose between living with a fault and undertaking major structural work. The latter course is infinitely more preferable if the stair faults are a hazard to the family.

Creaking treads
An irritating squeak can often be cured by applying talcum powder to the edges of treads and risers. The powder acts as a lubricant to lessen the friction between the timbers.

But if a tread not only creaks but can be felt to move when stepped on, the problem is more serious. A loose tread is almost always caused by a loose wedge or glue block beneath. This is particularly common in homes with recently installed central heating —as the timbers dry out, the wedges begin to lose their hold.

Exposed stairs
If the area beneath the affected part of the staircase is exposed, locate the wedges and test them for fit by wiggling them or tapping them lightly with a thin offcut of timber and a hammer.

Remove any loose wedges one at a time and inspect them for damage. If a wedge is warped or broken, cut a replacement from a length of 25mm square softwood, about 20mm longer than, but to the exact shape of, the original. Make sure that the new wedge and its housing are clean and dry, then apply some PVA wood-working adhesive to the wedge and drive it into place with a hammer (fig. 5). When the wedge is tight, leave it to dry, then trim off the end with a tenon saw (fig. 6).

If a removed wedge is intact, scrape

1 To cure a loose or creaking tread test the wedges glued into place beneath. Remove any wedges that are loose or damaged

2 If a wedge is warped or damaged, cut a replacement. Make the new wedge the same shape but about 20mm longer

3 Use an old chisel to chip out all the old adhesive in the housing. Make sure that both the housing and the wedge are clean and dry

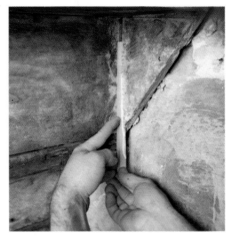

4 Coat the edges of the new wedge with some woodworking adhesive. Push the wedge upwards into place in its housing

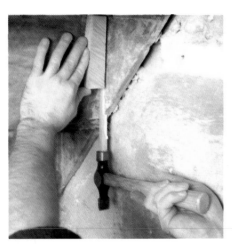

5 Drive the wedge with a hammer to make sure that it fits tightly. Hold a timber offcut against the wedge to prevent it from slipping

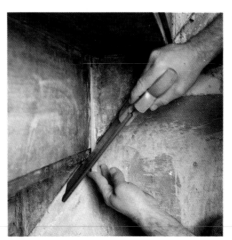

6 When the wedge is secure in the housing, leave it until the glue has set, then trim off the end with a tenon saw

7 If there are no glue blocks under the steps, secure loose treads by fixing metal brackets about 150mm in from each string

off any old, hardened glue and reglue it in place.

When all the wedges are secure, check the glue blocks (where fitted) and remove any loose ones. If screw fixing holes into the stairs have become enlarged, plug them before refitting the blocks. If the blocks have been nailed, it is worth replacing the nails with No. 8 (4.2mm) 32mm screws. Remove any hardened glue and make sure the surfaces are clean and dry before you reglue loose blocks.

If there are no blocks secure any loose treads by fixing metal brackets, a little shorter than the treads, 150mm in from each string (fig. 7).

Covered stairs

If the underside of the affected part of the stairs is covered with lath and plaster, access can be gained only by ripping out the plaster with a claw hammer and bolster. This is a time consuming and extremely dirty job, but worthwhile if the treads are particularly loose.

Fortunately, a loose tread can often be secured—though less effectively—from above. The joints between the top edges of the risers and the treads are sometimes held together by screws or nails. These may have become loose and need retightening.

Where no screws or nails are fitted, there may be a considerable gap between the treads and the top edges of the risers. New screws can be fixed if the treads are butt-jointed. In tongued-and-grooved joints use nails, as the slender parts of the wood in the joint might be weakened by screws.

To identify the type of joint, insert a knife blade into the gap between the tread and the riser. Where there is a moulded strip beneath the nosing, prise this off with an old chisel first. If the knife blade goes right through, it is a butt joint; if its path is blocked it is tongued-and-grooved. In some tongued-and-grooved joints the outside edge of the riser forms the front of the tongue, so there is no horizontal gap between the two.

To secure a butt-jointed tread, drill pilot holes for two countersunk screws through its top surface and into the riser, just behind the nosing. Position the holes about 150mm in from each string. Having countersunk the holes and driven in the screws, fill over the screw heads with wood filler. If the stairs are not carpeted, match the wood filler with the existing wood.

The steps of open-riser staircases, which are a feature of open-plan architecture, have no risers, giving them a modern airy look. The treads can be supported on wooden blocks attached to the inside faces or the top edges of the strings, or they can be fitted into housings cut into the sides of each string.

The treads of an open-riser seldom creak, because of their thickness and the more simple structure of the staircase. However, if they are housed into the strings, wood shrinkage may cause the treads to move in the housings.

If a housed tread creaks or can be felt to move, push it up in its housings from below and cut wedges to the rough shape of the areas in which movement is taking place. Coat the wedges with PVA adhesive and drive them firmly into the housings below the tread with a timber offcut and a hammer. Then, if possible, allow 24 hours before stepping on any newly wedged treads.

On some open-risers, a steel rod is fixed between the strings beneath every fourth or fifth tread. If treads seem loose, tighten the mounting screws of these rods.

Worn nosings

On old, uncarpeted stairs, years of use inevitably wear away the nosings—particularly in the middle. If a nosing is badly worn, it can be dangerous and should be replaced.

Prise off the moulded strip beneath the nosing (if fitted) and on a cut-string staircase, prise off the planted side nosing as well. Use a firmer chisel or a jig saw to cut back the edge of the nosing to an angle, then level the surface with a block plane (fig. 11). Do not cut the wood right back to the riser or the joint may be weakened, particularly if it is of the tongued-and-grooved type.

8 *If a nosing is badly worn, it can be dangerous. To replace a nosing mark out the area that is to be cut away from the tread*

10 *Do not cut the wood right back to the riser or the joint with the tread may be weakened. Remove the cut section from the tread*

Next, cut a piece of 38mm x 32mm softwood to the length of the exposed tread—on a cut-string, allow extra length for the mitre into the planted nosing—and then glue and nail it into place. When the glue has set, use a block plane again to shave the new piece to shape (fig. 16).

Where necessary, mitre the end of the new piece so that if fits with the edge of the planted nosing. If you want to make the new nosing more secure, fit countersunk screws and fill the ends with wood filler.

Worn treads

If the wear extends further back from the nosing, you can use a plane or chisel to level the surface. But bear in mind that if you remove more than 5mm of wood, you may seriously weaken the tread.

9 *Cut out the affected part of the nosing with a jig saw or a firmer chisel with a wide blade. Mitre the cut at each end*

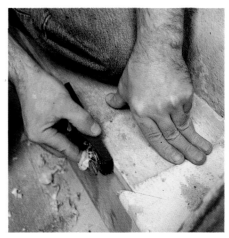

11 *Level the surface that has been cut with a block plane, then use a chisel to clean out any remaining fibres in the corners*

12 *Cut a new piece of nosing, to the length of the area, from a piece of 38mm x 32mm softwood. Hold into place and check for fit*

13 *Hammer the new length into place protecting it with an offcut of timber, then mark the shape of the nosing onto its edges*

A better alternative is to remove the nosing as above and fill the worn areas with a strong wood filler so that the surface is level. When the filler is dry, cut a piece of 6mm plywood to the shape of the tread and glue and pin it in place. Fit a new nosing to match the modified tread.

Loose newel posts

It is unusual for newel posts to cause any problems when securely fixed but if one becomes loose, it should be dealt with immediately as it is such a vital part of the structure.

To secure a loose post, first lift the adjacent floorboards (see pages 43-48). Tighten the bolts that attach the post to the floor joist and, if possible, reinforce the joint between the two by screwing wood blocks or metal angle brackets to the corners.

If the mortise-and-tenon joint between a newel post and the outer string is loose, the treads and risers can also work themselves loose, making the whole staircase potentially dangerous.

Use a 9.5mm drill to bore two holes into one side of the newel post, through the string tenon, and into the other side of the post. Prepare two hardwood dowels, 10mm longer than the holes, and coat them with PVA adhesive. Insert the dowels into the holes then, once the glue has set, trim the dowels so that they are flush.

The bottom step of a staircase—called the *curtail* step—often projects beyond the newel post and is separate from the rest of the structure. If it is badly worn, it can be replaced entirely, though you should make sure that the replacement is exactly the same height and width as

14 *Remove the new piece and, using the marks on its ends as a guide, plane it roughly to the shape of the existing nosings*

15 *Apply woodworking adhesive to the new nosing and drive it back into place. Nail the new nosing and punch the heads below the surface*

the old step or the altered slope may cause an accident.

If any other tread is particularly badly worn, or even cracked, do not attempt to replace it without first seeking professional advice. Where the treads and risers are tongued-and-grooved, or where a rough carriage is fitted, it is virtually impossible to remove a tread without dismantling the entire staircase.

However, where the underneath of the staircase is accessible, a cracked tread can be strengthened satisfactorily by fitting angled brackets at each side as shown in fig. 7.

Loose balusters and handrails

If the balusters are fitted into recesses at either end, they are unlikely to come loose. Often, however, they are cut at an angle at the top and just

nailed to the handrail. Where the lower side of the handrail is grooved, the spaces between the balusters are often filled by strips of wood glued and pinned into place.

To remove a loose baluster, prise out any filler pieces under the handrail and tap the top of the baluster in the upward direction of the staircase. If the baluster is fitted into a mortise at the other end, it should now be possible to pull it away. On a cut-string staircase, prise off the planted nosing and tap the baluster base out from the edge of the stairs.

With the baluster removed, clean both ends and glue a short block of wood on to the top edge. When the glue is dry, cut the block to the shape of the baluster and test it for fit between the rail and string. Trim the block to the correct length to make a

16 *Once the adhesive has set, use a block plane to shape the profile of the new nosing accurately. Then smooth the edge with glasspaper*

tight fit, then glue it back into place and replace any wood filling strips and the planted nosing, if fitted.

To secure a loose wall handrail, either fix longer plugs and screws to the loose brackets, or reposition the brackets and fill the old holes. Some people are tempted to remove the handrail altogether, but in some circumstances this is forbidden in the UK Building Regulations.

The handrail between newel posts, is either attached by mortise-and-tenon joints, or glued and nailed to the posts. Joints can be reinforced in the same way as those between the newel posts and outer strings, or, if the handrail is glued, fresh glue and new nails can be added. But if a handrail is loose, and the balusters are in a bad condition as well, it may be worth replacing the whole assembly.

Timber staircase construction

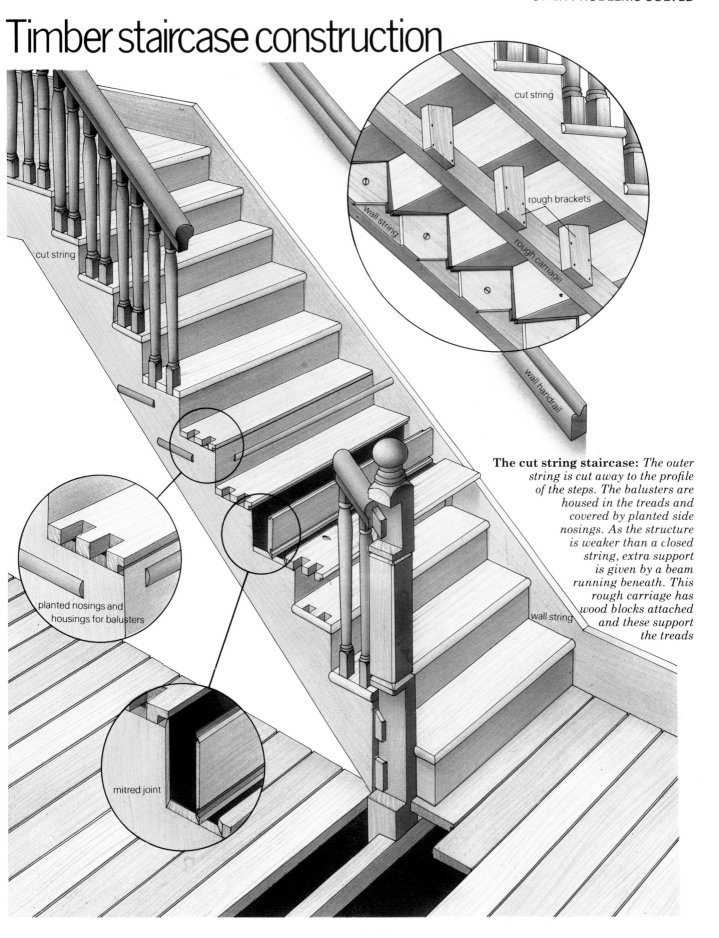

cut string

cut string

wall string

rough brackets

rough carriage

wall handrail

planted nosings and
housings for balusters

mitred joint

wall string

The cut string staircase: *The outer
string is cut away to the profile
of the steps. The balusters are
housed in the treads and
covered by planted side
nosings. As the structure
is weaker than a closed
string, extra support
is given by a beam
running beneath. This
rough carriage has
wood blocks attached
and these support
the treads*

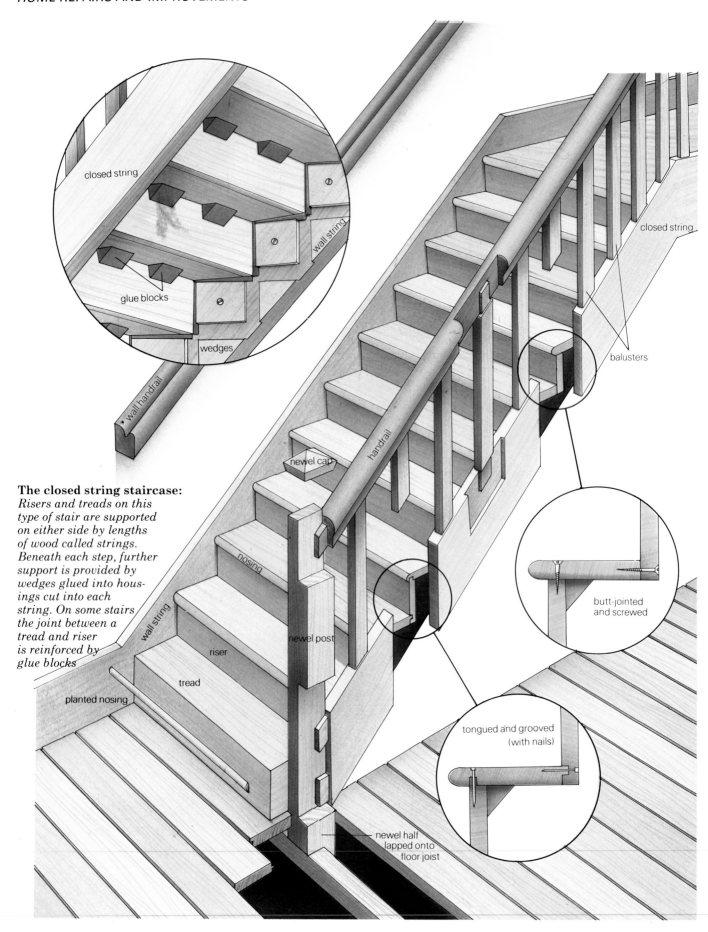

closed string

wall string

glue blocks

wedges

wall handrail

closed string

balusters

newel cap

handrail

butt-jointed
and screwed

The closed string staircase:
*Risers and treads on this
type of stair are supported
on either side by lengths
of wood called strings.
Beneath each step, further
support is provided by
wedges glued into hous-
ings cut into each
string. On some stairs
the joint between a
tread and riser
is reinforced by
glue blocks*

nosing

wall string

newel post

riser

tread

planted nosing

tongued and grooved
(with nails)

newel half
lapped onto
floor joist

DOOR REPAIRS

Hinging and rehanging a door successfully is easy if you follow a few simple rules. And even more complicated jobs, such as changing the direction in which a door opens, are not as hard as they seem

Below right: *This small kitchen is made even more cramped by a door which opens inwards. By rehanging the door to open outwards more space is immediately created in the kitchen and easier access provided*

There is nothing more annoying than a door which is difficult to open and close. And although the trouble can usually be put right quite easily, neglecting such a door may cause more extensive damage which is costly and difficult to repair at a later date.

Before attempting any repairs, it is worth considering what hinges are available and how you hang a door properly. Indeed, when a door hangs badly, the hinges are often at fault: either they are fitted badly or the wrong ones have been used.

Choosing hinges
Plastic, nylon, or—better still—pressed steel hinges are suitable for light internal doors, but if you are fitting hinges to a heavy, outside door, use the strong type made of cast steel. If you want a finish which is rust free, jam free and decorative, brass hinges look good but are more expensive and less durable.

By finding out the thickness, weight and height of your door, you can estimate what size of hinge you require. For example, a lightweight door, 32mm thick, would need a 75mm × 25mm hinge whereas a heavier door, 45mm thick, might require a 100mm × 38mm hinge. Be careful not to buy a hinge which is too wide for the door as this will result in a weak, narrow strip of wood where the hinge is fitted. To find the size of a hinge, first measure its length and then the width of one of its leaves to the middle of the knuckle where it swivels.

Most doors are fitted with butt hinges and you can buy either the fixed or the rising variety. The rising butt hinge allows the door to rise as it is opened but shut down closely on to a carpet or threshold as it closes. This means that though the door does not scrape against floor coverings, it will stop draughts and reduce fire hazards once it is shut.

Rising butt hinges are either right or left handed, so decide which way you want your door to open before you buy a set. Avoid confusion by getting the difference clear in your own mind.

Marking and fitting
Before you fit the hinge decide which side you want the door to open. Panelled doors can be hinged on either edge but most modern flush doors can only be fitted with hinges on one edge.

On some doors the hinge positions are marked on the edge of the door and these areas are usually reinforced, so it is advisable not to try to fix hinges to any other spots.

Once you have decided which edge of the door is to be hinged, arrange it so that it is resting on the opposite edge. Support the door by wedging it into a corner, cramping it to the leg of a table, or by holding it in a vice (fig. 1).

The best positions for the hinges are 215mm from the top of the door and 225mm from the bottom, but make sure that this does not leave them over any joints or the door may be weakened.

Use a marking knife and try square to mark the hinge positions on the door edge, starting from the knuckle edge where the hinge will swivel. Mark across all but 6mm of the edge then continue on to the face of the door, marking the thickness of one hinge leaf (fig. 2).

Next, open one of the hinges and lay it in position on the door edge to check that the lines you have drawn are accurate. Hold the hinge in position and use a marking knife to mark each end (fig. 3). Then scribe the width and depth of a hinge leaf on to the door edge and frame (figs. 4 and 5).

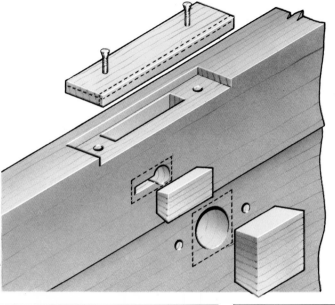
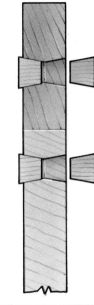

A. Left: *Holes left in the frame by relocating the lock, keyhole and handle need to be filled with wood*

Cutting out

The hinge recesses are now ready to be cut out. Use a bevel-edged chisel and start by chopping downwards across the grain in a series of cuts 5–6mm apart (fig. 6). Leave a thin uncut border of about 2–3mm around the three edges (fig. 6). Hold the chisel flat, bevel side up, and pare away the chipped-up timber. Finally, with the flat side of the chisel parallel to the door edge, clean out the recess.

The hinge should now press firmly into place flush with the surrounding timber. You may have trouble with some types of hinges which are bent due to pressure in their manufacture. If

1 *Before fixing hinges, stand the door on edge and support it securely with a vice firmly clamped to one end of the door*

2 *Position the hinges 215mm from the top of the door and 225mm from the base, keeping them well clear of any joints*

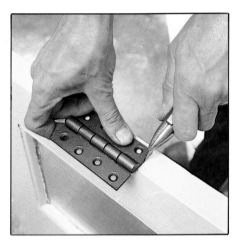

3 *Use a marking knife to mark the hinge position on the door edge. Make sure that the hinge knuckle is facing the right way.*

4 *Then set a marking gauge to the width of a hinge leaf and scribe this on the door edge between the two lines previously marked*

5 *Reset your marking gauge to the depth of one hinge leaf and mark this on to the face of the door frame between the two knife cuts*

6 *Use a bevel-edged chisel to cut out the hinge recesses. Make a number of cuts 5-6mm apart, to leave an uncut border around the edge*

this is the case, pare away a further 1–2mm from the recess.

Fixing hinges

Once the hinge is comfortably in position, carefully mark the screw holes with a sharp pencil then remove the hinge and remark the screw centres with a centre punch. Try to mark these a little off centre—towards inside of the recess—so that once the screws are inserted, the hinge will be pulled snugly into position (fig. 8).

Drill pilot holes to the depth of the screws and then clearance holes deep enough for the screw shanks. For heavy butt hinges use No. 7 or No. 8 × 38mm screws. Insert the screws so that they finish level with or slightly below the hinge plate (fig. 9).

If you are using brass screws, put in a steel screw first. This will cut a thread in the wood and avoid the possibility of shearing off or damaging the soft brass screw heads.

Fitting the door

Position the door in its frame by supporting the base with wooden wedges made from offcuts (fig. 10). Both door and hinges should be in the fully open position unless you are using rising butt hinges, in which case they should be closed.

With all types of hinge, make an allowance at the base of the door for any proposed floor covering and adjust the gap as necessary by altering the positions of the wedges. When you are satisfied that the door is in the right place, mark the position of the top and bottom of each hinge on the door frame with a pencil.

With the door removed from the frame, mark out the hinge recesses—their length, width and depth—accurately with a marking knife and adjustable try square. Use the same technique to cut the recesses as you used for those on the door.

Replace the door and position it exactly using the wooden wedges, then tap the hinge leaves into place in the waiting recesses. Finally, mark and pre-drill each screw hole, then insert one screw in each hinge so that you can check that the door opens and closes properly. If it sticks at any point, make minor adjustments by chiselling away more of the rebates before you drive home the remaining screws.

Sticking doors

If a door sticks and you can find nothing wrong with the hinges, it may be that part of the door frame has swollen. Where the swelling is slight and there is plenty of clearance between door and frame, investigate the possibility of bringing the swollen part away from the frame by either packing or deepening one of the hinge recesses. Be sure to make only the slightest adjustments in one go, or the door may stick elsewhere around the frame.

Where the swelling is more severe, you have no choice but to plane off the excess and redecorate the door. The planing can be done with the door in situ providing you first wedge the base to take the weight off the hinges.

Older doors and those particularly exposed to damp may warp or become loose at the joints, causing them to fit badly in their frames. In the case of

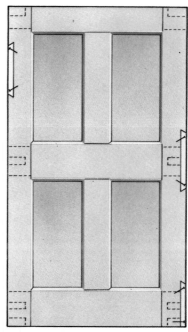

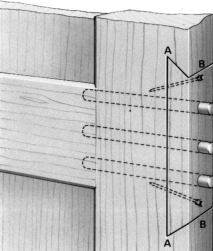

B. Right: *Badly weakened areas need to be cut out and replaced with dowelled sections. Start by cutting along line A-A, then B-A*

7 *Cut out the chipped-out timber in the hinge recesses with a chisel —held bevel side up—until the recess is clean and smooth*

8 *Mark the screw holes slightly off centre towards the inside of the recesses. This allows the hinge to bed securely once it is fixed*

9 *Once you have drilled pilot and clearance holes, insert the screws so that they are slightly below the level of the hinge plates*

10 *Wooden wedges made from offcuts can be placed under the foot of the door so that it can be positioned to fit the frame exactly*

11 *Broken or damaged joints can be strengthened by first drilling out the old wedges to a depth of 75mm using a 15mm twist drill*

slight warping, one answer is to make a small adjustment to one of the hinge positions so that you take up the twist. Do this on the frame—not on the door.

However, a more satisfactory solution is to remove the door so that you can cramp and strengthen the frame. Take off all the door furniture—the hinges, knob, lock, key escutcheon—place it flat on a workbench, then cramp the frame square using a sash cramp with a long bar.

Where gaps appear in the joints, scrape out any dust, accumulated grime and old glue with a chisel or knife. Then bring the joints together by cramping across the frame in two or more places. Use softwood offcuts to protect the door from being bruised by the cramps.

Next, drill out the old wedges holding the tenons at each frame joint to a depth of 75mm (fig. 11); use a 15mm twist drill bit. Make up some 85mm lengths of 15mm dowel with longitudinal cuts in them to allow for compressing (fig. 12) and chamfers at one end to give a snug fit.

Liberally smear each piece of dowel with external grade waterproof woodworking adhesive then drive them home into the drill holes with a mallet. Check that the cramps are still holding the frame square by measuring across the diagonals—which should be equal—and leave the adhesive to set. When it is dry, cut off the excess dowel with a tenon saw and finish the edges in the normal way.

Repairing a damaged stile or rail

If a stile or rail is split, it is usually possible to open this up, force in some adhesive then cramp it closed again. In this case, where necessary, place some

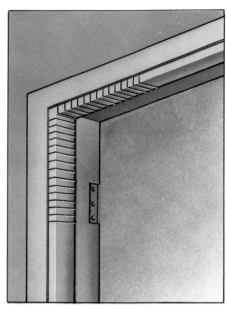

C. Above: *Remove a rebated door stop by first making a series of cuts around the corner of the frame*

newspaper between the split and the cramp protective offcuts to stop the latter from sticking to the frame. When the adhesive has set, fill any remaining cracks with wood filler and finish with a block and glasspaper.

Very badly damaged or rotten areas must be cut out completely and replaced with new timber. Using an adjustable bevel and marking gauge, determine and mark out the extent of the damage along the frame. Mark the width of the damaged area with a marking gauge on the face of the door.

You must now cut out the timber. In the example shown in fig. B, you would make the internal cuts A-A by drilling through the wood, then finishing with a

12 *The holes can be filled with glued 15mm thick dowels, chamfered at one end and with longitudinal cuts*

13 *When removing a planted door stop, first use a blunt, wide chisel and a mallet to prise the stop away from the door frame*

14 *By inserting the claws of a hammer into the gap, the door stop can then be worked loose and away from the frame*

padsaw or powered jig saw. Make the cuts B-A with a tenon saw, remove the damaged section, and smooth the cut edges with a wide, bevel-edged chisel.

Mark out and cut a replacement section, making it slightly wider than the frame so that it can be planed flush after fixing. Secure the section with woodworking adhesive and oval nails, the latter punched well below the surface level.

If the replacement section is over a joint, the tenon in that joint will have been seriously weakened by the repair. The remedy is to drive two or three dowels through the new timber into what is left of the tenon (fig. B). Drill and glue the dowels as described above.

Changing direction
It is often useful to change the direction in which a door swings—to make more space in a small room for example —or to hang it from the opposite side of the frame.

Making a door open in the opposite direction involves removing and resiting the door stop, altering the hinge rebates and possibly changing the door furniture. You may or may not have to change the hinges, depending on what type you have. Ordinary butt hinges can simply be used the other way up.

How you go about the job depends on whether your door stop is simply planted—nailed to the frame—or rebated into it.

Removing a planted stop: Remove the door from the frame and clear the space around you. Then use a blunt, wide chisel and mallet to cut into the joint between stop and frame and lever the latter away (fig. 13). The stop is bound to be securely fixed and you may have to use considerable force.

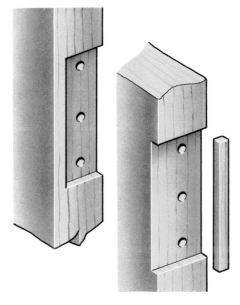

The job becomes easier when you can insert the claws of a claw hammer and ease the stop away, working upwards from the base of the door (fig. 14).

Once the door stop has given way, remove any old glue or chipped wood with a chisel, plane and glasspaper.

Removing a rebated stop: Start by measuring by how much the stop protrudes, then mark this amount down and around the outside face of the frame with a marking gauge.

Next, take a tenon saw and make a series of cuts 12–18mm apart in the top corners of the door frame (fig. C). Remove the waste between these with a wide chisel, with the door held firmly, and paring across the grain. This done, you can insert a rip saw or power saw and cut downwards through the remainder of the door stop. Afterwards, plane the cut timber flush with

D. Left: *When changing the direction of opening, the hinge recess has to be moved to the opposite edge*

the rest of the frame and use a chisel to clean up the corners (fig. 15).

Rehanging
When you come to rehang the door, the hinge recesses may well have to be moved. Do this by chiselling them across to the other side of the frame. Then make up wood blocks to fill the now unused parts of the recesses and pin and glue them in place (fig. D).

Refit the door stops—or make up new planted ones in the case of rebated stops—in accordance with the new door position. Make sure that the stops are firmly pinned and glued (fig. 17).

If the door lock or latch is handed, you must exchange it for a new one and fit it according to the manufacturer's instructions. Alter the position of the striker plate and make good the old recess as you did the hinge recesses. Finally, re-hang the door.

Changing sides
If you decide to change the side on which the door hangs, all the above operations will be necessary and you will have to swop over the door furniture to the other side.

As this is often handed, make sure that it is still suitable for the new door opening. Indeed, this is a good time to exchange the furniture for a new set.

Make good the holes left in the door by driving in tapered and glued wood blocks, cut oversize so that you can plane them flush with the surface. When you have done this, fill any remaining gaps with wood filler and repaint the door (fig. A).

15 *To remove a rebated stop, make a series of cuts around the corners. Chop out the waste and cut away the remainder of the stop*

16 *When rehanging a door which was hinged on the other side, pin pieces of wood block to fill the gaps and plane smooth*

17 *If the door is rehinged to swing in a different direction, a new door stop must be added so that the door will close properly*

Dealing with rattling doors

A rattling door is usually an indication that the timber has shrunk and the door no longer butts tightly up against the door stop. You may be able to cure the rattle with self-adhesive draughtproofing foam, but a better remedy is to reposition the striker plate on the door frame so it is a little nearer the door stop. This involves unscrewing the striker plate, enlarging it slightly and fixing it, using new screw holes.

If the door has also warped slightly along its opening edge and cramping is not effective in pulling it back square, the best solution is to mark the profile of the warped door edge on the door stop and then prise it off so you can plane it down to the line. Replace it so its planed edge meets the door surface snugly, then fill the nail heads and repaint the bare wood to complete the repair.

18 Close the door and measure the gap between the door and stop. Then mark this distance on the frame, measured from the edge of the striker

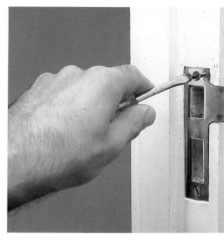

19 Unscrew the countersunk screws holding the striker plate in place along the door frame. Set the striker plate and screws aside

20 Use a straightedge (or the striker plate itself if you prefer) and a marking knife to indicate the edge of the new striker plate rebate

21 Next use a sharp bevel-edged chisel to enlarge the rebate up to the marked line. You may have to enlarge the latch and lock recesses

22 Test the fit of the striker plate, then screw it into position and test the operation of the door. Finally, fill the exposed edge of the old rebate

23 If the door is warped and cannot be cramped square, reshape the door stop. Scribe the profile of the door edge onto the stop

24 Lever the bottom edge of the stop away from the frame, starting at the bottom and working upwards. Pull out all old nails

25 Cramp the stop in a vice and plane the edge down to the marked line. Then nail it back to the door frame so the door fits against it

FIRST STEPS IN PLASTERING

Types of plaster ● Essential tools ● Preparing the surface ● Mixing the plaster ● Repairing a damaged section ● Applying the base coat ● Finishing off ● Patching corners

Above: *Plaster is applied to a wall with a laying-on trowel. When you are spreading plaster, keep the trowel's top edge tilted towards you.*

Plaster can be applied to solid surfaces, such as bare brick, cement rendered brick, building blocks or concrete, and to surfaces to which a key for the plaster—such as metal lathing or wooden slats—is attached. On most solid surfaces two coats of plaster, known as the floating coat or undercoat and the setting or finishing coat, are applied. When lathing is fixed to the surface, an additional first rendering coat is necessary called a pricking up coat.

Plasters

The main constituent of ready-mixed plasters is gypsum, calcium sulphate, which has been partly or wholly dried in a kiln. The extent to which the gypsum has been dried, and the addition of further constituents during manufacture, determine the type and grade of the plaster. However, as water is detrimental to gypsum plasters after they have set, they should not be used for external work.

Gypsum plasters, incidentally, should not be confused with cement render—a surfacing material made from sand, cement and lime and generally used externally. Render looks and feels like bricklaying mortar, which has similar constituents.

Lightweight, pre-mixed gypsum plasters are the most commonly used nowadays, by both professionals and amateurs. They come in several types, each used for a specific purpose.

Browning is a floating coat (undercoat) plaster used on semi-porous surfaces such as bricks, clinker blocks (breeze blocks) and concrete blocks.

Bonding is a floating coat plaster used on less porous surfaces such as poured concrete, where getting good adhesion is difficult.

Finish plaster is used for the thin surface coat that is applied over the undercoat.

Special plasters are also available for skimming plasterboard should this be required.

If in doubt on which undercoat plaster to use, ask the advice of your builder's merchant.

Always store plaster in a dry place. If any water comes into contact with plaster before it is used, the properties of the plaster will be altered. You should use plaster as soon as possible after buying, as the retarder—the

constituent which governs the setting time—grows less effective with time. Plaster is usually date stamped on the bag and, whenever possible, you should use the plaster within six weeks of the date.

Tools for plastering

Most of the tools you need for plastering can be made yourself. They include:

Spot board: This can be a piece of exterior grade ply about 1m² and is used for holding the mixed plaster. A couple of coats of exterior grade polyurethane wood lacquer will help to preserve the wood. The board should be placed on a stand—a wooden crate or sturdy stool will do—at a convenient height from the floor. The board should overhang the stand slightly so that the hawk can be held under the edge when transferring the plaster on to it.

Hawk: A board about 300mm × 300 mm for carrying plaster from the spot board to the work area and for holding the plaster as you work. Professionals use aluminium hawks with moulded-on handles, but you can get by quite comfortably with a home-made one. Cut your square from an offcut of timber or plywood and screw on a handle about 200mm long cut from 50mm × 50mm timber with the edges rounded off.

Laying-on trowel: Used for applying and spreading the plaster. It has a rectangular steel blade about 280mm × 120mm attached to a wooden handle. Some trowels have curved handles

Tip from the trade

Q **My cellar wall is of unplastered brickwork, painted over with gloss paint. Can I plaster it, or must it be dry-lined with battens and plasterboard first?**

A You can plaster painted walls, provided you first paint them all over with a thick coat of PVA adhesive, applied neat. Then you apply bonding and finish plaster in the usual way. The walls, however, must be dry and the paint adhering firmly, so experiment with a small area before you commit yourself.

which are easier to grip. A trowel of good quality is important as it is hard to obtain a smooth finish with a worn or inferior blade.

Gauging trowel: Available in a variety of sizes and used for repairing areas too small to be worked with the laying-on trowel. It is also useful for mixing small quantities of plaster.

Skimming float: Used for levelling the floating coat. Plastic skimming floats, light in weight and non-warping, are available. But you can make a serviceable float from a smooth, flat, straight-grained piece of wood about 280mm × 120mm × 10mm, with a wooden handle.

Scratcher: To ensure the adhesion of the next coat of plaster, the surface of an undercoat is scratched over. A suitable scratcher can be made by driving a few nails into a piece of wood and then cutting off their heads with a pair of pincers or pliers.

In addition, you will need two buckets—one for mixing the plaster in and one for holding water—a distemper brush and straight-edged rules of various lengths depending on the size and nature of the job. Also required, for chipping off old plaster, are a hammer and a bolster.

Preparing the surface

Before you start, clear the room of furnishings as much as possible, as the plaster dust will fly everywhere and can scratch polished surfaces. Cover what you cannot remove with old dust sheets. Have ready a suitable receptacle for the old plaster.

If the wall behind the plaster is of new brickwork it will need only brushing down and damping with clean water before you start to apply the new plaster.

Concrete wall surfaces require special preparation as their smoothness provides a poor 'key' for plaster and their density gives low suction. Before you plaster, paint the concrete with a PVA adhesive such as Unibond, applied neat.

Mixing the floating coat

When mixing plaster of any type use only water that is fit for drinking. Any impurities in water may be detrimental to the properties of plaster.

Pre-mixed lightweight undercoat for plastering small areas should be mixed a third of a bucket at a time. This is sufficient to cover a patch of about 300mm × 300mm to a depth of about 10mm. If the area to be plastered is larger than this, it is better to mix further amounts later. Pour water into the bucket first, then add the

1 Before you begin to replaster a patch, use a hammer and bolster to cut straight lines round the area. This makes plastering much easier.

2 Scrape some of the mixed plaster from the spot board onto the hawk with the laying-on trowel. Then trim off any excess plaster

3 Hold the laying-on trowel at an angle over the hawk and tilt the hawk slightly in order to snatch up a manageable amount of plaster

4 Hold the trowel against the wall surface, keeping its upper edge tilted backwards at an angle of about 30°. Draw it upwards over the patch

5 Apply further undercoat plaster until the patch is filled in and the new plaster is level with the old surrounding plasterwork

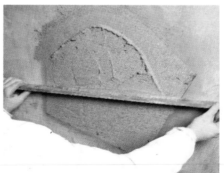

6 Take a straight-edged length of wood that is a little longer than the patch and draw it upwards to make the plaster flush with the edges

7 Use the laying-on trowel to trim away any excess undercoat plaster around the edges of the patch and on the surrounding wall area

plaster. If the plaster is put in first, it clogs when the water is added and sticks to the bottom of the bucket. Add the plaster, while stirring the mixture with a stick, until a stiff but workable mix is obtained.

Whenever you have finished mixing any plaster, pour it onto the spot board. Then clean the bucket out immediately, or any remaining traces of plaster will set and then be extremely difficult to chip off. Traces of old plaster in the bucket will also speed up the setting time of subsequently mixed coats.

Applying the floating coat

Mix the floating coat plaster and place it on the spot board. Hold the hawk beneath the overhang of the spot board—if you are right-handed hold the hawk in your left hand and vice versa. Use the laying-on trowel to scrape some plaster onto the hawk then trim away any excess (fig. 2). Tilt the hawk and 'snatch up' a small amount of plaster onto the trowel (fig. 3). Keep the trowel horizontal until the edge connects with the wall,

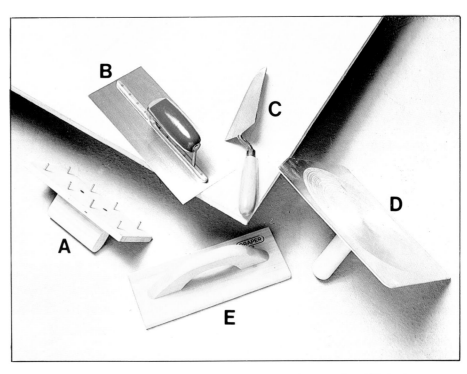

Above: *Tools for plastering include (A) home-made scratcher (B) laying-on trowel (C) gauging trowel (D) hawk, and (E) skimming float*

8 *To make room for the final coat of plaster, run over the surface of the undercoat using the skimming float to flatten and cut it back*

9 *Draw the straight-edge across the patch once more to check that the undercoat surface is level and lower than the surrounding plaster*

10 *Run the scratcher lightly across the undercoat surface to form ridges. This keys the surface, ensuring that the finishing plaster adheres*

11 *Mix up the finishing plaster and apply it to the patch using the laying-on trowel. Use firm pressure and upward strokes*

12 *As the finishing plaster begins to set, dampen it slightly with the distemper brush. Take care not to use too much water at this point*

13 *Wet the laying-on trowel and smooth it over the surface in circular movements. Finish off with light, upward strokes*

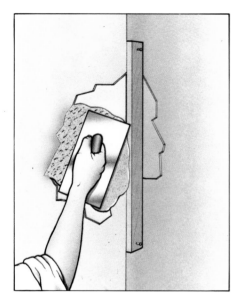

Above: *If a patch has to extend round a corner, nail a thin piece of batten to one side of the corner and plaster up to it*

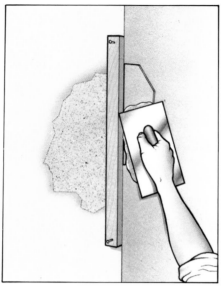

Above: *When the plaster is dry, remove the batten and pin it to the replastered edge. You are then ready to replaster the other side*

Tip from the trade

Q My newly-applied plaster keeps cracking, I think because the old, porous plaster is drawing the water out of it. Is there a remedy?

A Yes. Mix one part of PVA adhesive with four parts of water. Paint it onto the exposed brickwork and thoroughly soak the edges of the existing plaster. You should hear a 'fizzing' noise as the plaster soaks up the mixture; if not, the mixture is too rich. Apart from forming a water barrier, this treatment helps stiffen the old plaster.

then tilt the outer edge upwards until it is at an angle of about 30° to the wall (fig. 4).

Begin in the centre of the patch and work upwards, exerting slight pressure. Keep the laying-on trowel at an angle, with its upper edge clear of the wall, so that plaster is fed to the wall all the time (fig. 5).

If the patch is 10mm deep or less, fill it until the new plaster is level with the old surrounding plaster. If the patch is more than 10mm deep, do not attempt to fill it in with one coat as this results in the plaster shrinking back from the edges and cracking. Instead, fill the area to half its depth, then use the scratcher to key the plaster with criss-cross lines. Apply a second layer of plaster when the first layer is dry.

Now, take a straight-edged rule a little longer than the patch and, working from the bottom upwards, draw the rule from side to side over the plaster to make it flush with the edges (fig. 6). Fill in any hollows with more plaster and draw the rule over the surface again.

To make room for the finishing coat, the plaster in the floating coat must now be cut back to a depth of 2mm lower than the surrounding plaster. First, flatten and cut back the floating coat with the skimming float (fig. 8). Next, run the scratcher over the surface of the floating coat to provide a key for the finishing coat (fig. 10). Then, go over the plaster with the skimming float again to flatten the

burrs left by the scratcher. The scratch marks should remain but their edges should not protrude too far.

Clean the surrounding wall area to remove any adhering plaster and leave the floating coat to set. Ready-mixed plasters take between 1½ and 3 hours to set.

Before mixing your finishing coat, clean all tools and the spot board.

Mixing the finishing coat

Lightweight finishing plasters are applied thinly so they can always be mixed in a bucket. Pour water into the bucket until it is about a quarter full. Slowly pour in the plaster until it appears above the water and stir with a stick. Once the plaster has settled, add more and keep stirring until the paste reaches the consistency of thick cream. Then pour it onto the spot board.

Applying the finishing coat

Lightweight finishing coat plaster dries very quickly. So until you are experienced, mix and apply only enough to cover a small area at a time. Scrape some plaster from the spot board to the hawk and lift a small amount with the laying-on trowel. Use firm pressure to apply the plaster, using upward strokes as much as possible (fig. 11).

When the finishing coat is level with the existing plaster at the edges, draw the straight-edge over it until it is flush, filling in any hollows. As the plaster begins to set, dampen it with the distemper brush (fig. 12) to keep it

workable while you trowel it smooth. Do not use too much water as this can kill the gypsum plaster in the surface and cause crazing. Wet the laying-on trowel and, keeping it as nearly flat as possible, run it over the surface in circular movements, finishing off with light upward strokes (fig. 13). If you do not achieve a smooth, flat surface at the first attempt, dampen the surface and try again.

Patching corners

If a patch extends around an external corner, nail a batten with a smooth, straight edge to one side of the corner so that its edge is level with the existing plaster on the other side. Plaster up to the corner so that the new plaster is flush with the edge of the batten.

Tip from the trade

Q After every plastering job, I seem to finish with half a bag left over. Must it be thrown away?

A No. On its own, it will become unusable within days of being opened. But if you mix it with a proprietary cellulose filler (such as Polyfilla) you can use it for filling holes in plaster up to about 150mm across and 12mm deep. Use three parts of plaster to one of filler, and add water to make a fairly stiff mix. Unlike the cellulose filler, it will not 'slump' out of the hole. Kept dry, plaster for this purpose will keep for about six months.

REPAIRING GUTTERS AND DOWNPIPES

Gutters and downpipes play a vital role in protecting your house from the effects of rain. But unless guttering is regularly maintained it will deteriorate, causing leaks or overflows. The damp in turn causes structural damage which often costs a fortune to repair

All guttering systems should be inspected twice a year, in late autumn and again in the spring. It will almost certainly be necessary to sweep out any accumulation of leaves and dirt with a hand brush and trowel or, in the case of plastic guttering, with a shaped piece of hardboard.

Keep the debris well away from the outlet leading to the down pipe. If the outlet does not have a cage or grille fixed to prevent debris from entering and blocking the downpipe, roll a piece of galvanized wire netting into a ball and insert it in the neck of the pipe. Do make sure that the wire ball is sufficiently large not to fall down the pipe.

With cast-iron or galvanized iron guttering, check carefully for any rust. Use a wire brush to remove loose flakes of paint and rust and treat the surface with a rust inhibitor. The surface should then be given one or two coats of bituminous paint to form a strong protective layer.

On Ogee-section guttering (fig. A), or galvanized guttering fixed on with through spikes, rust may well be found around the fixings to the fascia—in which case the damaged section may have to be removed for treatment on the ground.

Basic safety

In order to reach the gutters for a close inspection, you will have to rig up some form of access and in most cases this means using a ladder. If you haven't already got a ladder, you shouldn't have any trouble in hiring one from your local tool hire shop.

When using a ladder, it's as well to be aware of a few basic safety rules. First, don't lean the ladder against the guttering itself or the fascia which may not be able to take the weight. If you can, hire a ladder stand-off which clips to the rungs and holds the ladder away from the wall. Secondly, make sure that the foot of the ladder stands square and firm on the ground—the base should be placed out from the wall by a quarter of its height. And thirdly, never work from the very top of a ladder—you'll have nothing to hold on to and it's easy to lose balance.

Left: *Clearing a downpipe. A blockage in a downpipe can cause the system to overflow with damaging results*

1 *Leaves and debris soon accumulate in gutters, especially during the autumn. Clean them out with a trowel or stiff brush*

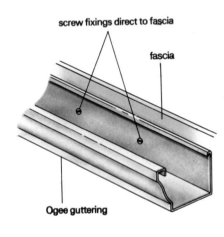

A. *Guttering of Ogee-section is often screwed directly to the fascia boards*

Sagging gutters

If a gutter sags, water may overflow or the joints may crack and leak. A bucket of water poured in at the highest point of the system reveals any such defects.

The commonest causes of sagging are broken or bent brackets, or loose fixing screws or spikes. Most guttering is supported on brackets screwed either to the fascia boards underneath the eaves of the roof (fig. C) or to the ends of the roof rafters.

To rectify a sagging gutter, remove the defective sections and examine the brackets to see if they are firmly fixed. If they are not, use longer screws to secure them. Where brackets are bent or corroded, replace them with matching new ones.

Replacing a rafter bracket (fig. D) normally involves removing the roof covering directly above it, though this problem can often be overcome by fixing a fascia bracket adjacent to the faulty rafter bracket to give the necessary extra support.

Ogee section guttering differs from other types in that it is screwed or spiked directly on to the fascia. Sagging here is usually caused by the fixing devices rusting and then pulling away from the fascia. In this case, plug the holes and re-fasten with new screws or spikes.

A common fault with guttering occurs where the slope or fall towards the downpipe outlet becomes distorted —because of faulty installation or settlement of the house itself. Too steep a fall causes water to overflow at the downpipe outlet. Too shallow a fall results in a build up of water and sediment along the run.

To determine the correct fall for an incorrectly aligned section, tie a length of twine along the top of the gutter—from the high end to the outflow point—and use it as a guide to reposition the intervening supports. The gutter should fall 25mm for every 3m of its length.

Leaking joints in cast-iron

The joints in cast-iron gutter systems are held together by nuts and bolts which are usually screw-headed. A proprietary sealing compound—often a mixture of putty and red lead or a mastic sealer—is sandwiched between the two ends to make the joint watertight (fig. D).

A leaking joint may be patched up by cleaning the area with a wire brush and applying one or two coats of bituminous paint. However, for a more permanent repair the section on one side of the leaking joint must be removed, cleaned and replaced. If the removed piece is in the middle of a run, two new joints have to be made—one at each end of the section.

Start by removing the bolts which hold the joints together. These may well have rusted and seized—in which case apply penetrating oil to loosen them. If this fails, saw through the bolts with a junior hacksaw. With Ogee-section guttering, remove the screws holding the section to the fascia as well.

Lift out the loosened section—making sure as you do so that its weight does not catch you off balance —and take it to the ground (fig. 3). Returning to the guttering, chip off all traces of old sealing compound from the hanging end (fig. 4) and scour it thoroughly with a wire brush. Repeat the cleaning operation on the removed section (figs. 5 and 6).

Apply fresh sealing compound to the socket section of the joint, spreading it in an even layer about 6mm

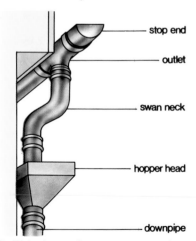

B. *This downpipe connects to the gutter run via a swan neck*

stop end
outlet
swan neck
hopper head
downpipe

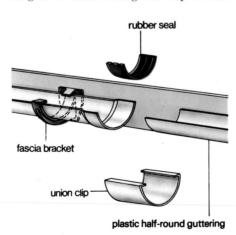

C. *A section held by a fascia bracket. This joint type is sealed in the socket*

rubber seal
fascia bracket
union clip
plastic half-round guttering

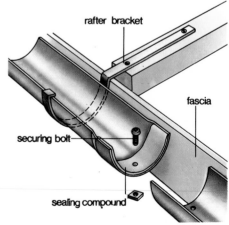

D. *A joint in cast-iron guttering. The gutter is supported by rafter brackets*

rafter bracket
fascia
securing bolt
sealing compound

2 *This leaking section of cast-iron guttering is on the end of a run. The guttering is secured by screws in the fascia rather than by brackets*

3 *When the bolt in the joint at the other end of the section has been loosened and removed, you can pull the section away from the wall*

4 *The leak is at the joint with the adjoining section. Using hammer and screwdriver, gently chip off traces of old sealing compound*

5 *Repeat the cleaning operation for the section that has been removed. Scrape off old sealing compound from the joint end*

6 *When the old sealing compound has been removed, scour clean the two ends of the joint thoroughly with a wire brush*

7 *Apply new sealing compound to the socket section of the joint, spread in an even layer about 6mm thick over the socket area*

8 *Having replaced the removed section and fitted the joint together, take a new bolt and insert it in the hole in the joint from above*

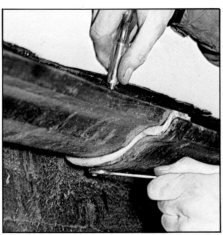

9 *Screw the securing nut onto the end of the bolt and tighten with screwdriver and spanner so that joint closes and squeezes out compound*

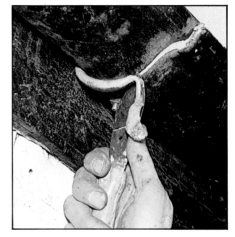

10 *Use a putty knife to trim away all excess sealing compound squeezed onto the surface above and below the gutter*

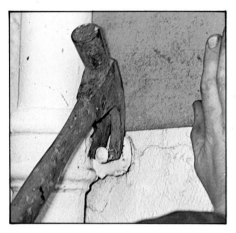

11 *This cast-iron downpipe is fixed to the wall by pipe nails driven into wooden plugs which have loosened. Remove the nails with a claw hammer*

12 *With the pipe nails removed, pull away the lower section. Joints sealed with compound will have to be loosened first*

13 *Having dug the loose plugs out of the masonry, extend the holes with a 12mm masonry drill to make sure replacement plugs fit*

14 *Using a hammer, firmly drive your replacement wooden plugs into the holes until they are flush. Make sure the plugs are firm*

15 *When both plugs have been fitted, replace the lower section so that the bracket holes are level with the plugs. Hammer in two new nails*

16 *To prevent the downpipe cracking, force some fresh jointing compound into the joint, then wipe it smooth with a rag*

thick (fig. 7). Relocate the removed gutter section, screwing it to the fascia or laying it on its brackets and fitting the joints together.

Insert a new galvanized bolt into the joint from above (fig. 8). Screw on its securing nut, tightening gently so that the joint closes up and squeezes out any excess compound (fig. 9). Trim away the excess with a putty or filling knife (fig. 10), wipe over the area with a damp rag, then repeat the operation for the other joint. Finally, repaint the joints with one or two coats of bituminous paint.

Replacing a cast-iron section
If the whole system has eroded, it may be advisable to replace it with plastics guttering.

However, if the rest of the run is still in good condition, replacing a corroded cast-iron section is well worthwhile.

Where possible, take the old section to a builder's merchant and obtain a matching replacement. As well as the shape and diameter, check that the new section matches the existing joints. If not, buy the appropriate union at the same time.

Cast-iron guttering is normally sold in 1.8m lengths, so the new section may have to be cut to fit. When measuring it up, take into account any overlap for the joints or new joint unions.

To cut it, lay the old section over the top of the new and use it as a guide. Mark the new section in pencil and lay a strip of masking tape along the mark, towards the waste side, to give a clearer guide. Cut the section with a large hacksaw.

Mark the positions of the joint bolt holes and punch and drill them to a diameter of 8mm before you fit the new section into place.

Leaking joints in plastics
Leaks from plastics guttering can be just as damaging as those from cast-iron and should be attended to as soon as possible.

In most plastics guttering systems, the sections are connected by union clips, lined with replaceable rubber seals (fig. E). In some cases, the seal is positioned in the end of one section of gutter with a separate clip used to secure the joint (fig. C). When the clips are sprung home, the gutter ends compress against the pad to form a watertight joint—but this can leak if silt finds its way in.

To replace a seal, undo the clip holding the ends together, lift out the

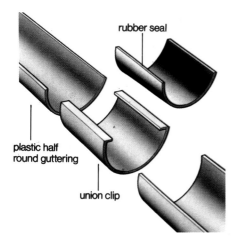

E. This section of plastics guttering is connected by a sealed union clip

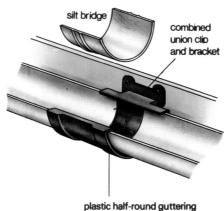

F. The joint in this gutter is sealed by a silt bridge clipped into the union

Tip from the trade

Q **What is the easiest way to cut roof gutter without the hacksaw wandering off line?**

A With awkward profiles like gutters, always turn the workpiece upside down so that your cut starts on one smooth surface, not on two projecting edges. To guide the saw, lay another length of gutter with a 'factory-made' end over the first and sight down the saw blade. It may also help to cut alternately from either side.

old seal and thoroughly clean the surfaces which come into contact with it. Fit a new seal of the same type and clip the joint back together by squeezing the ends of the gutter slightly and snapping the union clip over each edge of the section.

On systems which use combined union brackets, silt bridged joints are used (fig. F). The silt bridge clips into the union to prevent debris working its way into the joint and causing leaks. Leaks in such joints will be due to cracks—either in the bridge or in the union bracket itself—and can be

remedied by replacing the defective part with a matching new one.

To fit a new silt bridge, hook one end under the front of the union clip and snap the other end under the lip at the back of the gutter.

Cast-iron downpipe repairs
Cast-iron downpipes are usually attached to walls by pipe nails driven into metal, lead or wooden plugs. The nails run through cast metal brackets (fig. 11) some of which have spacers behind to prevent contact between the pipe and the wall. Brackets often come

loose, making the pipe dangerous.

To secure a loose bracket, start by removing the bracket nearest to the ground and repeat the operation up to and including the bracket that is loose. To remove a bracket, lever out the nails with a claw hammer (fig. 11). check that they are firm, then refit the downpipe (fig. 15).

In many houses, downpipe joints are unsealed. If dirt collects in an unsealed joint, water may gather and freeze and crack the pipe. Avoid this by filling any unsealed joints with a mixture of red lead and putty or a proprietary mastic. Wipe it smooth with a rag (fig. 16) then seal the joint with a coat of bituminous paint. Do the same with sealed joints that have become loose, having first chipped off the old compound.

Use an offcut of timber held against the wall to obtain the necessary leverage. Withdraw the section of corroded downpipe. Where the joints have been sealed and do not fall away easily, heat them with a blow lamp to loosen the sealing compound or chip the compound away by hand.

Remove the loose plugs by digging them out of the masonry, and make up replacements—slightly larger all round than the holes—from pieces of 12mm dowel. If necessary, extend the holes with a 12mm masonry drill (fig. 13). Drive the replacement plugs into the wall until they are flush (fig. 14).

Plastic downpipe repairs
Plastic downpipes are comparatively light and are less likely to work loose. However, if they do, they can be secured following the same procedure as for cast-iron downpipes. Sections of plastic downpipe are joined by socket and spiggot connectors.

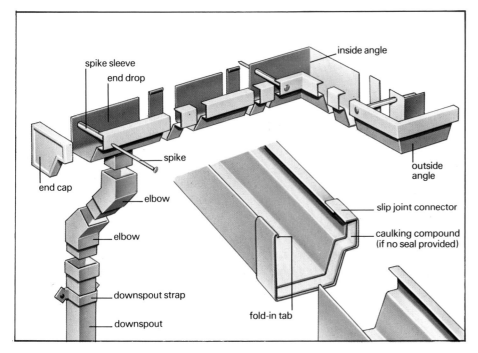

G. Snap-together metal gutters come in several patterns, and in plain or enamelled aluminium or galvanized iron. Take an old section with you

when you buy a replacement length to ensure the pattern matches. If there are no rubber seals where sections join, use plenty of caulking compound

17 *Hopper heads are notorious for collecting leaves and rubbish. Lift out as much loose debris as possible—try not to push it down*

18 *Force out a blockage in a straight downpipe with a stout rod. If there is a bend in the pipe, try pulling out the blockage with wire*

19 *Wash out any residue with a strong jet of water from a garden hose. To prevent further blockages, cover with mesh*

Replacing an enamelled section

Gutters made from thin-section aluminium or galvanized steel, finished with white baked-on enamel, are less subject to rust than cast-iron gutters. But they are apt to dent sometimes just by your leaning a ladder against them.

The procedure for replacing a damaged section is much the same as for plastics. First, jam a block of wood inside the gutter while you draw the fixing spikes with a claw hammer, and disconnect the damaged section at the nearest joints. Cut the new section with a hacksaw, using the old one to measure the correct length, and file off the burrs on the cut edges. If you are using spike supports, drill holes through the new section to receive them.

Next, clean off the old sealing compound from the undamaged sections, as described above. Fill the joint connectors with sealing compound, slip them into place, and fit the new gutter section, spiking it into place. Finally, bend over into the gutter the top ends of the connectors if these are designed with fold-over tabs.

At external corners, as with other types of gutter, you need two fixing spikes—one into each length of fascia.

Clearing blocked downpipes

Before unblocking a downpipe, put a plastic bowl or large tin under the base of the pipe at the discharge into the drain to prevent any debris entering the drainage system.

When cleaning hopper heads (fig. B), use rubber gloves to protect your hands against sharp edges.

To clear a blockage in a straight downpipe, tie a rag firmly to one end of a long pole and poke it down the pipe. Once the blockage has been dislodged, flush the pipe thoroughly with a hose.

If the downpipe is fitted with a hopper head carefully clear by hand any debris which has collected. Try not to compress the debris, or it may cause further blockage in the downpipe.

With plastic hopper heads, wipe the inside with a cloth and soapy water once the debris has been cleared.

With some systems, the guttering is positioned some way out from the wall and water is directed into the downpipe through an angled section known as a *swan neck* (fig. B). To clear a blockage here, use a length of fairly stiff wire in place of the pole so that the bends may be negotiated. With wire it's best to pull out debris.

If a blockage is beyond reach, the lower part of the downpipe will have to be dismantled.

H. *Modern rainwater systems are nearly always made from plastic which doesn't rot and last virtually indefinitely. The weak points in a plastic system are the joints but in most cases it is possible to buy and install replacements. The sections that you are most likely to have to replace include the following.* **A.** *Stop-end outlet.* **B.** *Coupling clip.* **C.** *Running outlet.* **D.** *Angle piece.* **E.** *Support bracket.* **F.** *Stop-end.* **G.** *Three-piece swan neck.* **H.** *Downpipe bracket. When buying replacement parts, check that they are compatible with the existing system.*

Old cast-iron rainwater systems (inset) usually follow a different plan in that they have hopper heads to collect the water that drains from the gutter. Because cast iron is heavy and corrodes easily, the weak points are often to be found around the support brackets **(I)** *which have pulled away from the wall*

REPOINTING BRICKWORK

Left: *Repointing is essential to protect the brickwork if the old mortar is crumbling or missing*

The mortar joints in brickwork protect a wall from the damaging effects of rainwater. So if the mortar shows signs of decay, replace it with fresh mortar to make a new seal

As long as brickwork is correctly designed and well built, it does not require much in the way of maintenance or repair work. But, as a building ages, the mortar joints between the bricks may begin to decay and crumble. Flaking joints in brickwork allow water to penetrate the wall and should never be neglected. The remedy for crumbling joints is repointing—clearing out the old mortar a short way and replacing it with fresh mortar to make a new waterproof seal.

Types of joint
The mortar between bricks can be finished in one of several ways; wherever possible, you should try to match new joints to the existing ones. However, if the old mortar is particularly badly decayed, you may not be able to see what type of joint has been used. In this case it is worthwhile making new weather-struck joints (fig. C).

The horizontal joints of this type have sloped surfaces which are slightly recessed below the upper brick and slightly overhanging the lower one. This slope allows water to run off quickly and prevents it from lodging on the lower edge of the joints, thus giving the wall further protection from rain and moisture. The vertical joints slope from one side to the other and match the angle of the horizontals above and below. Other types of joint commonly used in brickwork include:

Flush joint: When the mortar has almost dried, it is rubbed over with a piece of wood or old sacking to produce a surface flush with the surrounding brickwork (fig. E). This type of pointing looks particularly effective when used in conjunction with smooth-surfaced bricks.

Keyed or round joint: This is produced by running along the surface of the mortar with a semi-circular piece of metal to form a shallow, curved depression (fig. B).

Recessed joint: This is formed by scraping out the freshly-laid mortar to a depth of about 6mm below the brick surface, then smoothing the surface of the remaining mortar with a piece of wood the width of the joint (fig. D). Recessed joints look best on rough-textured bricks but should be used only where they match the existing pointing. If used on external walls in cold climates, the bricks must be hard and durable, otherwise water may collect and freeze on the ledges causing pieces of brick to flake off.

Equipment
For repointing brickwork, even if you are working over quite a small area of wall, you need a spot board on which to mix the mortar and a hawk for carrying the mortar to the work area (refer to page 73). For applying the mortar to the joints you need a pointing trowel, which resembles a small bricklayer's trowel, and for clearing out the old mortar use a shave hook with its pointed end cut off square.

If you are constructing weather-struck joints, you also need a *frenchman* for trimming away the excess mortar at the bottom of the horizontal joints. A suitable frenchman can be made from an old kitchen knife. Use a hacksaw to cut off the end of the knife, smooth off any burrs around the cut with a file, then heat the tip and bend it into a right-angle about 12mm from the end.

To guide the frenchman neatly along the joints when trimming, you need a straight-edged piece of timber which is held immediately below the top edge of the lower brick. Attach two pieces of hardboard to each end of the piece of wood so that when it is held against the wall, there is a slight gap allowing the trimmed mortar to fall through (fig. A).

Wherever possible, the mortar for repointing should be mixed to match the composition of the existing mortar. If you do not know the mixing proportions of the original mortar, use a $1:\frac{1}{2}:4\frac{1}{2}$ (cement:lime:sand) mix or 1 part of masonry cement to 3 parts of sand. An exception to the rule is the softer type of facing brick, where you should use a weaker mix; a proportion of 1:1:6 is more appropriate here.

Use as fine a grade of soft sand as possible, also called builders' or bricklayers' sand.

Working considerations

Repointing is generally best undertaken during warm weather as newly laid mortar is easily damaged by frost. However, avoid working in very hot weather, which dries out the mortar.

If you are working on a high wall, set up a platform or suitable scaffolding, so that you are working at chest height. Never be tempted to carry out pointing work standing on a ladder: you will not be able to reach the joints properly and you may fall.

If the area to be pointed is large, tackle the work in stages, finishing off the joints over an area of about 2m² before moving on to the next. Start work at the top left hand corner of the wall and move across and downwards.

Mortar for pointing should be mixed in small batches and then used immediately, thus preventing waste. If you do mix too much, and some begins to dry out and harden before you come to use it, discard it and mix a fresh batch. Do not try to reconstitute hardening mortar by adding more water to it.

Preparing the surface

If there is paving below the wall to be repointed, lay down a large sheet of polythene before you start work to protect the concrete path from stray mortar droppings.

With the protective sheeting in place, gently scrape any lichen and moss from the surface of the brickwork, taking care not to damage the faces of any bricks.

When the brickwork is clean, start raking the joints, using the shave hook or a plugging chisel, to a depth of between 12mm and 20mm—if you clear out the mortar further than this, the wall may be damaged. Rake out the vertical joints—called *perpends*—first and then the horizontal, or *bed*, joints again taking care not to damage the bricks.

Make sure that the recess formed in the joints is absolutely square and that no traces of old mortar remain on the edges of the bricks (fig. 1). If you fail to remove all the old mortar, the fresh mortar will not adhere properly and will soon flake and crumble.

When all the joints in the area to be repointed have been raked out, brush them thoroughly with a stiff scrubbing brush to remove any remaining particles and dust (fig. 2).

In order to prevent too much moisture being absorbed by the surrounding brickwork from the fresh mortar, dampen the wall by flicking

1 To prepare the surface of brickwork for repointing, rake out the joints a short way with an old shave hook

2 Make sure that no traces of old mortar are left at the edges and brush down the joints to remove any remaining dust

3 Dampen the surface of the brickwork with a distemper brush and clean water to make sure that the new mortar will bond

4 Mix up your first batch of mortar taking care not to prepare too much. Try to match the colour of the mix with that of the old mortar

thoroughly clean water over the surface with a distemper brush (fig. 3). However, take care not to use too much water or you will soak the brickwork and the fresh mortar will not adhere properly.

Handling the trowel

Opinions vary on the best way of using a pointing trowel, so it is best to experiment until you find a style that suits you before you start.

You may find that the easiest method is to roll the mortar down the hawk and divide it into 'strands'—as long as the trowel and about 12mm thick. Pick up each strand on the back of the trowel, along one edge, and flick it firmly into the waiting joint.

Weather-struck joints

Although slightly more difficult to construct than other types of brick joint, weather-struck joints are well worth the extra trouble as they give the wall added protection against water penetration.

To fashion weather-struck joints, start by transferring a manageable amount of mortar from the spot board to the hawk and carry it to the work area. Using the pointing trowel, force some mortar well into the first few perpends. Use the trowel to form a sloping angle by drawing it down the edge of the brick on the right hand side of the joint, then cut off the excess mortar neatly with the edge of the trowel (fig. 7).

Move on to the bed joints above and below the filled perpends. Holding the trowel point upwards, press in more mortar, so that it is recessed to a depth of about 3mm at the top of the gap and slightly overhangs the edge of the brick at the bottom.

5 *Transfer a manageable amount of mortar to the hawk and divide it into strands as long as the trowel and about 12mm thick*

6 *Carry the hawk to the work area and pick up strands of mortar with the back of the pointing trowel. Force the mortar into the joints*

7 *If you are making weather-struck joints, form the sloping angle in the perpends by drawing the trowel down the edge of the brick*

8 *Tuck the mortar into the beds of weather-struck joints so that it is recessed under the top brick and slightly overhangs the lower one*

9 *Trim off the excess mortar at the bottom of the weather-struck joints with a frenchman, then brush the joints to remove waste*

10 *If you are making recessed joints use a shave hook, with its point cut off, to scrape out the freshly laid mortar*

When you have used up the first batch of mortar, make the rough slope already formed in the perpends neater by trimming off any remaining excess with the pointing trowel so the mortar is recessed 3mm on the right hand side.

Next, take the frenchman and straightedge to the wall. Holding the straightedge immediately below the lower edge of the bed joints, run the frenchman along the wall, with its tip pointing downwards, to cut off the excess mortar (fig. A).

When the mortar has begun to harden, rub the joints with a dusting brush to remove any remaining waste then move on to the next section.

Flush and keyed joints
Pointing brickwork with flush joints provides a neat finish and can be particularly useful on old brickwork

where the outer corners of the bricks have crumbled and the wall surface is to be redecorated.

Start as for weather-struck joints by filling perpends then bed joints. Press the mortar firmly into place with the pointing trowel, until it protrudes slightly out from the surface of the brickwork.

When the mortar starts to harden, rub along the joints with a piece of wood or old sacking working in the same direction, until the mortar is flush with the surrounding brickwork (fig. E). When completely dry, scrape over the mortar with a stiff piece of plastic to remove any excess particles of mortar dust.

To form a keyed joint, press the mortar well into the joints with the trowel, then smooth it to shape with a semi-circular piece of metal—an old metal bucket handle or a small piece

of metal piping are ideal for this task. Marginally less efficient is a piece of stout rubber hose. After rubbing the joints, trim the surplus mortar at the edges with the trowel.

Cleaning the brickwork
Although all the joints should be cleaned off as thoroughly as possible during the pointing process, it is difficult to achieve a completely clean finish by this means alone and some mortar will probably be left adhering to the edges of the bricks.

Never try to remove mortar which has been spattered on bricks while it is still wet, or attempt to wash it off with water. Instead, leave the excess mortar to dry out completely then use a stiff scrubbing brush to brush the soiled bricks. Remove large lumps of mortar on clay bricks by scraping with the side of a trowel. With calcium silicate bricks, lightly abrade the surface with a brick of the same colour to remove large pieces.

If marks still remain on the brickwork because the mortar has penetrated the surface, they can be removed with a very dilute solution of hydrochloric acid—1:10 by volume for clay bricks and 1:2 by volume for calcium silicate. Saturate the brickwork with clean water, then apply the solution sparingly with an old paint brush, taking great care not to get any on your skin or in your eyes. When the area has been thoroughly treated, hose down the brickwork to remove every trace. The surface of some types of brick can be affected by acid so, if in doubt, consult the brick manufacturer before embarking on treatment of this kind.

Colouring joints

To produce a matching or decorative effect in finished brickwork vegetable dyes, proprietary colourants and spe-

A. *To trim the excess mortar from the bottom of the weather-struck joints, use a frenchman and draw it along the top edge of a straight length of timber held just below the top edge of the lower brick. Attach a thin block of wood to each end of the timber to let the trimmed mortar fall through the gap. Make a frenchman from an old kitchen knife*

cial coloured cements are all available from builders' merchants and can be added to the mortar mix if desired. But because the colour will be altered by the texture of ordinary sand, you should use white sand in the mix, if possible. Remember also that cement with colour additives requires less water than is normally used.

If you use a vegetable dye, the final colour will be a lighter shade as the colour pales as the mortar dries; experiment first with small measured quantities of mortar and dye and allow them to dry out. When you have obtained the required shade in one of the experimental batches, mix up your first full batch and add the dye in an equal proportion.

If you are repointing part of a wall and want the colour of the fresh mortar to match that in the existing joints, rub the joints around the area with candlewax to prevent them from absorbing the colouring in the new mortar mixture.

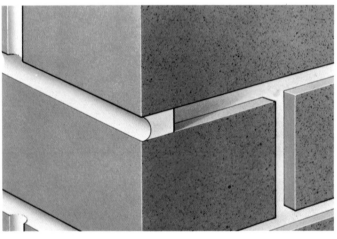

B. *Keyed joints are formed by smoothing the surface of the mortar with a rounded piece of metal*

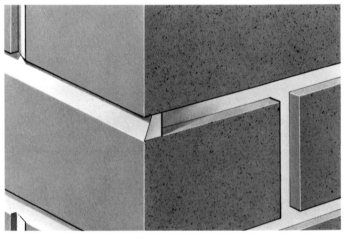

C. *The slope of weather-struck joints allows water to run off quickly, protecting the wall from rain*

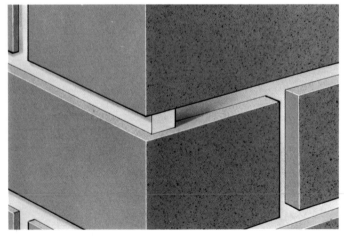

D. *The mortar in recessed joints is scraped out to a depth of about 6mm below the brick surface*

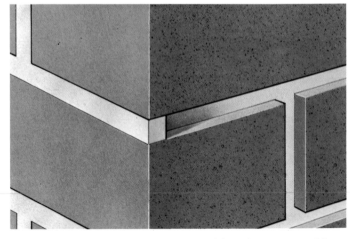

E. *Flush joints are produced by rubbing the mortar with a piece of wood to form a smooth surface*

INSTALLING A ROOF WINDOW

● **Planning a roof window conversion** ● **Window designs** ● **Tools and equipment** ● **Preparatory work** ● **Marking out and cutting an opening** ● **Fixing the window in place** ● **Fixing U-type and L-type flashings**

Below: *Installing a roof window is an economical and practical way of adding light and ventilation, enabling you to open up space in the home—such as a loft or attic—which might otherwise go to waste*

Parts of the home like the space under the roof are often under used—simply because of the lack of light or ventilation. Installing a roof window gets around these problems and enables you to create an extra room with a minimum amount of work—without the need for major structural alterations to the house.

Although roof windows are most usually fitted in attics, their use is by no means restricted to the main roof of the house. They can just as easily be installed in garage, shed or extension

roofs providing the pitch of the roof is somewhere between 20° and 85° and the timbers are sound.

Planning a roof window

You will almost certainly need building regulations approval for a roof window —this means drawing up plans of your proposals and submitting them to your local council. You may also need permission under the planning regulations, which are different from building regulations: see the panel overleaf for details.

If you simply want to introduce more light and ventilation into an attic which is already used as a room, then obtaining the necessary permissions is relatively straightforward. But if you want to convert an ordinary attic into a habitable room the procedure is more extensive. From the planning point of view, you will be creating an extension, which may or may not require planning permission. From the building regulations point of view, you will have to make sure the attic will satisfy the regulations for a habitable room—for

Regulations

Get information on building regulations and planning permission from your local authority. Briefly, both sets of regulations can apply even if you are not carrying out any structural work, but are merely changing the use of a room—for example, converting a loft into a habitable room.

Building regulations are concerned with ensuring that buildings are constructionally sound. Regulations vary from country to country; contact your local authority to find out what applies to you.

Planning laws exist to ensure that what you do is environmentally acceptable. In both the UK and Australia, the work of converting a loft may not need formal approval under the planning laws—but again, check with your local authority first.

example, it must have sufficient ventilation and insulation, enough headroom; and a strong enough floor. Converting your loft in this way is a major undertaking, and you may prefer to enlist professional help.

Since the weight of even the largest roof window is spread over a wide area, the rafters do not have to be particularly wide; but they should be at least 100mm deep. Check also that they are well seated at the eaves and at the apex of the roof by standing near the middle of each rafter and shaking it vigorously. If you detect excessive movement, the rafters concerned must be strengthened and reseated before the window is installed in the roof.

Choosing a roof window

Recent developments in the design of roof windows have greatly extended the range and effectiveness of the old-style 'skylight'. This consisted of a simply constructed metal- or wood-framed window, hinged at the top and opened and closed by means of a long handle attached to the bottom of the fixed frame.

By contrast modern roof windows are usually double-glazed and hinged centrally on both sides, allowing the sash to pivot through 180° for easy cleaning and maximum ventilation. They can be fitted with locks, and also with integral ventilation flaps and blinds which open and close between the double glazing.

1 Start by measuring the external dimensions of the frame and transfer these measurements to the outside of the rafters

2 Check the thickness of the trimmers and measure this distance up from your top mark and down from the bottom mark

3 Then, to allow for the splay, use a level to draw horizontal and vertical lines from your top and bottom marks respectively

4 Remove tiles well clear of the marked-out area, starting from the centre and working slowly towards the outside

5 With the roof covering off, erect temporary supports and then remove the rafter by cutting at the lines previously marked

6 Fit trimmers across the frame and check they are correctly aligned before nailing them to the adjoining roofing timbers

7 *To complete the frame, carefully mark the position of the false rafter on the trimmers. Cut this and then fix it in place*

8 *Cut a slot in the battens and place the frame on the outside of the roof. Mark the frame's position and then withdraw it*

9 *Using the marks made on the outside of the roof as a guide, cut back the battens. Allow enough clearance for the flashings*

For roof windows which are out of reach, and therefore difficult to open and close, electrically-operated models are available. And for areas which are hemmed in, an emergency exit window can be fitted which pivots both sides—like the ordinary model—and along one edge to allow easy escape.

Once you have decided on the type of model most suited to your needs, take care to choose the size which gives optimum light and ventilation without looking unduly large compared to the room in which it is fitted. As a rough guide, the area of the window—including any air bricks—should be at least 10 percent of the floor area of the room. Another important point to bear in mind is that two small windows can often be used

instead of one large one. Such an arrangement gives as much ventilation and light as one window but can avoid the need to cut through rafters during fitting (fig. B).

Because a roof window is more exposed to the elements than a window mounted on a vertical wall, it is usually protected with flashing around the outside of the frame. This is supplied with the window but before purchasing, check that you have the flashing compatible with your particular type of roof. Two types are available: U-type flashing for profiled roofing such as tiles, and L-type for thin or flat roofing materials such as slates or bituminous felt.

Essential equipment

Very few specialized tools are necessary to fit a roof window successfully and you will probably have most of them already. To mark out the area to be removed you need a tape measure and a pencil or felt tipped pen as well

10 *Reposition the frame and check it carefully for squareness. Then screw the angle brackets into the rafters at each side*

as a spirit level and plumbline. A sharp handyman's knife is necessary to cut away any felt which might be on the roof under the covering.

Many tiles or slates are difficult to prise loose—particularly if they are firmly nailed—and a small plasterers' trowel or slate ripper will make this task easier. A panel saw (hand saw) is needed to cut the rafters and battens once the tiles or slates are removed.

Once the window is set in place a screwdriver is needed to fit the side profiles securely. Then, to ensure that the flashing is flattened against the surrounding tiles or slates a lead dresser or soft-faced hammer is useful. Finally, to trim and shape the roofing material to fit around the window you need slate cutting tools and pincers, plus a supply of fixing nails.

B. Below: *Careful positioning of two small roof windows* (right) *can often reduce a great deal of the work involved in installing one large roof window* (left)

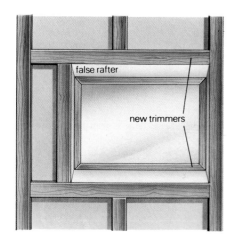

false rafter

new trimmers

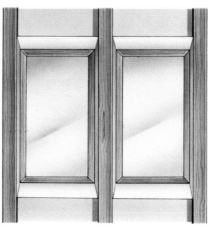

11 *Next fit the bottom flashing section into place and secure it by slotting the bottom profile over the top and screwing it tight*

12 *Next fit the side flashings and secure them by adjusting the sliding clips so that they can be nailed into one of the battens*

13 *To support the top flashing, fill the gap above the frame with battens spaced at 20mm intervals and nailed across the rafters*

14 *Then slide the top and side profiles into position and fix them securely with screws to the frame below*

15 *Finally, clip the top flashing into place and make sure that it is firmly attached to the top profile you have just fitted*

16 *Check all connections for tightness and then dress the bottom flashing—made of pliable lead—against the roof covering*

Preparatory work

Although all of the work involved in installing a roof window can be safely carried out from inside, it is very easy to drop tiles and timber on unsuspecting passers-by. So, before you start work, cordon off the area immediately below where you are working with clearly marked signs and improvized barriers.

If fitting the window involves cutting away rafters, prepare for this before you start work. To support the ends of each severed rafter, make up two pieces of timber long enough to stretch from the floor and cut the top ends at an angle to fit the rafter slope at top and bottom.

Once the rafters are cut through, timber noggins—called trimmers—of the same dimensions as the existing rafters are fixed at top and bottom across the gap to strengthen the frame. Prepare for this by measuring the distance between rafters that will accommodate the width of the window.

Next, unpack the window and remove the wooden sash by rotating it through 180° as if you were opening it. This will expose the hinges so that you can fully tighten the retaining screws and lift the frame away.

Strip the sash free of all metal components except for the two aluminium profiles near the hinge—most can be screwed loose then pulled free. Check that all the woodwork is clean and free of defects then give it a protective coat of polyurethane lacquer, allowing this to dry before starting work on the roof; further coats can be added later.

Positioning the frame

You may already have a good idea where you want to install the window but check this exactly at this stage by lifting the frame into position against the roof. Take into account that you will want the control bar within easy reach at the top of the window and perhaps also a view from where you are likely to be sitting.

Once you have worked out the exact position in which you want to fit the window, measure its outside dimensions and carefully transfer these on to the rafters with the help of a spirit level (measurement 'A' in fig. C). Align the base of the marked-out area with the bottom of a course of slates or tiles—this will help to fix the flashing more neatly once the window is in place.

17 Replace the tiles or slates down both sides, trimming them to size so that they fit neatly under the edge of the flashing

18 Then replace the top ones, leaving a gap of 60–100mm above the window. Fit a tilting fillet to support a short bottom course

19 Once the roof covering is complete, carefully pick up the sash (taking care not to break the glass) and fit it into the frame

20 Check that the window opens and closes easily. If it sticks, retighten all the screws and make sure the sash is correctly aligned

Next examine the installation instructions supplied with the window. These specify the clearance required between the frame and the roofing material to ensure a neat fit. Take careful note of the dimensions, marking them onto the roof timbers in a different colour if necessary, so that you know how many tiles or slates to remove (measurement 'B' in fig. C).

Note also that the trimmers which need to be inserted above and below the frame to give it support are not tight against the frame itself: they are set further back to enable the internal window linings to be splayed and so allow a greater spread of light.

First check the thickness of your trimmers and measure and mark this distance above and below the frame position to allow for their width

(measurement 'C' in fig. C). Then allow for the inner splay, using a spirit level to draw horizontal and vertical lines from your new top and bottom marks respectively to the inside of the rafter (measurement 'D' in fig. C). It is at these points that the rafter will be cut and the trimmers nailed into position.

Cutting an opening
Once you have rechecked that the inside of the roof is correctly marked out, start to remove the roofing materials. How you proceed depends on both the structure of the roof and its covering:

Tiles and slates: Start by cutting away any internal roofing felt with a sharp handyman's knife so that you expose the tiles or slates themselves.

Remove these one at a time, starting from the centre and working slowly towards the outside (fig. 4). If they are nailed to the battens, work each tile or slate free with a slate ripper or wedge a trowel under the top edge to break it loose. Continue in this way until you have a space well clear of the area to be occupied by the window.

Felt roofs: Using the marks you have made on the inside on the roof as a guide, drill a 20mm diameter hole right through both the wooden decking and the covering felt. Then insert a padsaw and carefully cut around the outside of the marked-out area. When the cut is completed, the inside of the area will drop away and can be lifted clear of the working space.

Once you have removed the roof covering, the next step is to cut away any rafters running across the area to be occupied by the window. But before you do so, make sure that they are supported at top and bottom with timber wedges, placed well away from the area in which you intend to work (see above).

Saw each rafter along the two lines previously marked, trying to keep the cut at the correct angle to the roof. Then prise the freed section away from the roof, taking care not to break or damage any of the battens or roof timbers (fig. 5).

To take the place of the missing rafters fix your trimmers across the top and bottom of the frame. Check carefully that these are correctly aligned with the existing roof timbers and square at each corner before nailing them securely through the uprights and on to the ends of the cut rafter (fig. 6).

With the trimmers set above and below where the frame is to go remove the temporary support and fix a false rafter down one side. Fit this according to the installation instructions so that there is a gap on each side of the frame to allow for the roofing material. Cut the rafter to length, check carefully for alignment and square, then nail it firmly to the trimmers top and bottom (fig. 7).

The window frame should now be placed on the outside of the roof and checked for fit. Do this by sawing down through the centre of the battens or sarking so that you have a slot wide enough to allow the frame to be pushed through sideways (fig. 8). When the frame is on the roof adjust its position exactly—remembering that you will have to replace all the roofing materials around the outside once it is fixed. When you are satisfied that it is

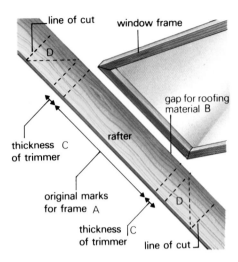

C. Above: *Take great care when marking out the height of the frame (A), clearance for roof materials (B) thickness of trimmers (C) and the internal splay (D)*

set exactly as you want it, mark this position on the roof battens underneath (fig. 8).

While the frame is still in place, locate the four angle brackets and screw them to the outside of the frame—two on each side. Use the line marked on the side of the frame as a guide and adjust the position of the brackets accordingly to ensure a watertight seal once the window is in place. The line should coincide exactly with the top surface of the battens or sarking.

Once you are satisfied with these adjustments, take the frame back inside and replace the roof covering up to the bottom of the marks made for the frame. Make sure you do this exactly so that the frame can be set back into position without gaps between it and the surrounding roofing material. Use pincers to nibble away sharp corners along the top of the tiles or slates so that the flashing is not damaged once it is applied—especially along the bottom edge.

Next, you must cut back the battens using the marks you have made on the outside of the roof as a guide. But study the installation instructions before doing so since the exact position of the cuts varies according to whether you are using U- or L-type flashing (fig. 9).

Set the frame back in position and check the clearance at all sides, adjusting as necessary by cutting away more of the battening or adding small battens where there is too large a gap. Afterwards, check that the frame is square by measuring both the

diagonals and along the outside edges (fig. 10). Then secure the frame by screwing the angle brackets into the rafters at each side.

With the frame firmly held, fit the bottom flashing section into place and secure it by slotting the lower frame profile over the bottom of the window and screwing it tight (fig. 11). The rest of the flashing should then be fitted.

Fixing the flashing

The technique used to fit the flashing and ensure a weathertight seal around the window, depends on whether you are using U-type flashing for a profiled roof or L-type flashing for a flat or slated roof:

U-type flashing: Fix the side flashings first. They have a raised lip along the edge furthest from the window to hold the tiles at a correct

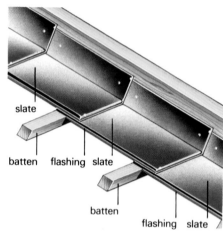

D. Above: *Flat or slated roofs are made watertight by laying pieces of flashing under the roofing material*

distance from the frame, so check you have them the right way round. The side sections are secured with clips ready-fitted to them. Locate these and nail them to the battens below (fig. 12), then fix the bottom section in the same way.

The gap above the frame must now be filled to provide good support for the top flashing. Do this by nailing a number of battens across the rafters spaced at about 20mm intervals (fig. 13). Then replace the top and side profiles by sliding them into place and screwing them to the frame (fig. 14). Finally, clip the top flashing into position, making sure that it is firmly attached along its bottom edge to the top profile you have just fitted (fig. 15).

With all the flashing in place, double-check that it is fitted correctly and that all of the screws are

tightened around its outer edges. Then, using a lead dresser or a soft-faced hammer, flatten the bottom flashing—which is made of soft pliable lead—against the roof covering as shown in fig. 16.

When you are satisfied that the flashing is fitted so as to give an all-round weatherproof finish, replace the tiles or slates around the outside. Start with those on each side of the frame, trimming them to size so that they fit neatly just under the edge of the flashing (fig. 17). Then replace the top ones, leaving a gap of 60–100mm above the window depending on where the bottom course finishes. If you have to cut across the tiles or slates to establish this gap—and so end up with a bottom course of shortened tiles—fit a tilting fillet of wood below the bottom course before you fix them in place (fig. 18).

L-type flashing: Secure the bottom flashing section—which should already be in place—by fitting the lower frame profile and screwing it tightly to the frame. Then fill the gap above the window with wooden battens, spaced at roughly 20mm intervals and nailed into the rafters, so as to provide a solid base for the flashing and roof covering above the window.

The roof on each side of the window is then made watertight by fixing the short sections of flashing—called soakers—to the edge of the frame with nails and alternating these with slates or pieces of roofing felt. Start at the bottom edge of the frame and fit a soaker. Lay a slate on top of this and then another soaker and continue in this way until you reach the top (fig. D). Depending on the size of the window, the top soaker may have to be cut to length in order to fit below the top slate.

Once the sides of the window are made watertight, fit the top frame cover and side profiles and screw them down firmly. Finally, replace the slates or felt above the window so that the top frame is slightly overlapped. The window and its surrounds should then be checked to ensure that they are fitted correctly and screwed tightly in place.

Replacing the sash

Refit the sash into the frame and make sure that it is firmly held. If you have fitted it correctly and the frame is square, the window should open and close easily. But if it sticks, check that all screws are tightened and that the sash is correctly aligned before trying again.

INSTALLING AN EXTRACTOR FAN

Positioning a ventilator

You can mount an extractor fan (exhaust fan) in a convenient external wall or window. Either way, it should be located as close to the ceiling as possible, near the sink and stove but not right above these unless the window or wall here is high.

Window mounting requires that a hole be cut in the glass. Although not a difficult task (see overleaf) accidental breakage is all too easy. Using a replacement pane with a hole cut in it by the glazier makes fan installation much easier.

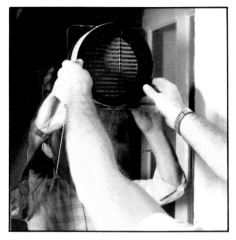

A. *When the hole has been cut, fit the flange and gasket assembly of the unit in place. The components screw together with this unit*

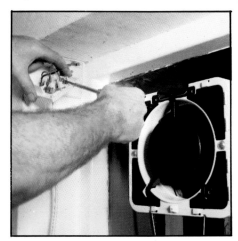

B. *A fused spur needs to be wired to a junction box situated close to the fan. Conceal the wire using plastic ducts to the junction box*

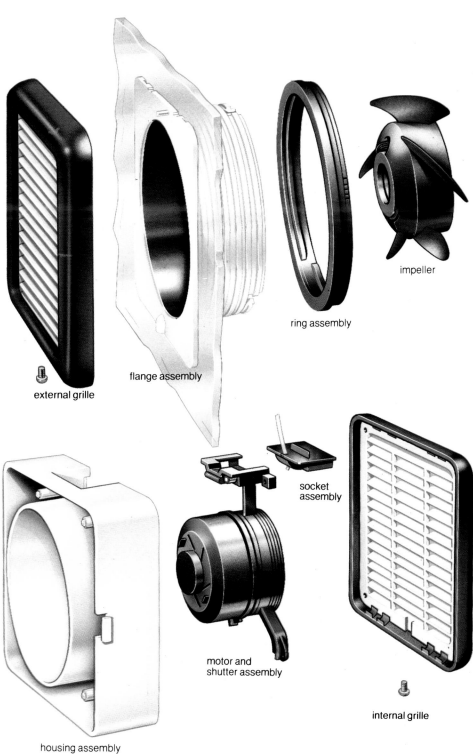

external grille

flange assembly

ring assembly

impeller

socket assembly

motor and shutter assembly

internal grille

housing assembly

Above: *This unit is typical of a number of extractor fans for domestic use. As with others, the design is based on a number of interchangeable components, which enables straightforward assembly and maintenance. Flange and ring arrangements — each with gasket — are screwed together to fix the unit in place*

A plywood board, holed and trimmed to size, can be used instead of glass, but needs to be of exterior grade plywood and to be well sealed or painted. This is really only suitable where you are replacing a small window pane.

The appeal of window mounting is that no structural work is involved. Offset against this is the obstructed view, restricted window opening for summer time ventilation and the appearance of the unit.

It takes a little longer to install a wall-mounted fan but the additional effort is usually considered worthwhile. The necessary removal of inner and outer brickwork is not a difficult job for the handyman, especially with the small areas involved here.

The hole should not be made any nearer than two bricks' lengths to a wall edge otherwise structural weakening may occur. In the case of a cavity wall, a liner must be used to seal off the cavity or fumes and moisture will be expelled into it.

C. *After you have completed the wiring, fit the face-plate by snapping it into place on the lugs provided on the box*

Extractor fans are also used to give ventilation to internal rooms. Do not be tempted, though, to have the outlet

D. *Pull-cord switches hanging from the extractor fan allow you to operate the fan conveniently, and with safety*

from a fan discharge into an unused chimney flue—this is likely to cause condensation problems.

Cutting a hole in a window

It is generally easier to replace an old pane with a new one ordered from your glass merchant, who will cut the hole for you. However, this may be expensive if the pane is large, and in this case try to cut the hole yourself.

Before doing this, clean the glass on both sides to ensure a clean cut. Then hire a circle glass cutter, which has a sucker base plate and a trammel arm along which the cutter slides. Set the cutter position to give a circle of the required diameter, and draw out the resulting circle on a piece of card so that you can check its size.

You will also need an ordinary glass cutter to criss-cross the cut-out, plus a pair of pliers and a pin hammer.

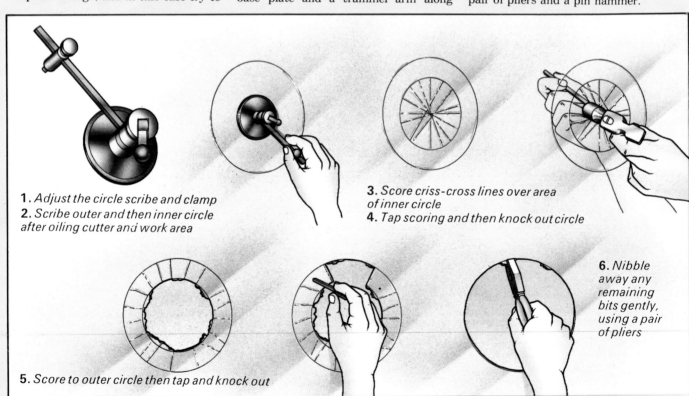

1. *Adjust the circle scribe and clamp*
2. *Scribe outer and then inner circle after oiling cutter and work area*

3. *Score criss-cross lines over area of inner circle*
4. *Tap scoring and then knock out circle*

6. *Nibble away any remaining bits gently, using a pair of pliers*

5. *Score to outer circle then tap and knock out*

REPAIRING ROOF FLASHINGS

● **What flashings are** ● **The choice in repair materials** ● **Basic repairs** ● **Bending metals** ● **Using flashing tape** ● **Using semi-rigid mineral fibre** ● **Repairing straight flashings, corners and valleys** ● **Mortar flashings**

A. Above: *Self-adhesive flashing tape is the simplest to use of all flashing materials and is usually first choice for basic repairs. The tape comes in rolls, together with its own bituminous primer*

External flashing is the term given to the watertight joints between partially separated structures on a house, such as a chimney stack and its surrounding roof area, where a roof butts up against a wall, or where dormer windows and rooflights have been introduced.

Quite simply, it is one of the most vital defences against penetrating damp. Yet, during the regular course of household maintenance and repair, flashing is probably more often neglected than anything else—until, of course, damp patches start to appear on chimney breasts, in the loft or on bedroom and attic ceilings.

In fact, it is a simple process to maintain and repair flashing. Regular checks on its condition should be made from inside the house and are best accomplished in between spells of heavy rainfall. A loft inspection—around the underside of roof valleys and where a chimney stack enters the

roof space—will soon reveal telltale signs of water entry.

Look for water stains on the roof timbers and trace them back to their source. The stains might be yellow, brown or almost black in colour and will appear as streaks along the timber. If the roof covering is slate, the streaks may be white. And if the leak is an old one, fungus might also be present in the form of wet rot.

Searching for leaks can sometimes prove difficult in the confines of a roof space, but you can use a mirror attached to a long pole to help you see under eaves and other difficult areas. Follow up your search by scanning the outside with binoculars.

It is essential that you trace leaks right back to their source. For example, water seen to run down the underside of a valley board does not necessarily mean that the valley liner is at fault. Careful investigation might reveal that the leak is in the

ridge capping and that water is running down a rafter and then on to the valley board.

The flashing on older UK houses is usually made from either lead or zinc, but it is quite common to find other reasonably corrosion-free materials in use—such as duralumin, copper, bituminous felt and semi-rigid mineral fibre (the latter sold in the UK under the trade name Nuralite).

For the do-it-yourself enthusiast, the introduction of self-adhesive flashing has enabled speedy and effective repair work to be carried out. Self-adhesive strip can be purchased in a variety of widths from most hardware stores and consists of heavy duty aluminium foil, sometimes coated with grey lacquer to resemble lead, and backed with a bitumen adhesive. This adhesive surface is protected with siliconized releasing paper which you simply peel off prior to applying the flashing tape itself.

Basic repairs

Generally, the most common damage you will find to flashings are small cracks and, sometimes, tears. And these can be rapidly repaired with either self-adhesive flashing strip or bituminous mastic.

Before attempting to cover the crack, the surrounding area must be thoroughly cleaned with a fine wire brush and emery paper. And where self-adhesive flashings are to be used, the sub-strata must be treated with a special primer prior to fixing. Manufacturers' instructions generally say that this is only necessary when applying the flashing to porous surfaces such as brickwork. But when applied to metals such as lead, aluminium or copper, it stops the metal oxidizing and you will find that this makes for easier and more effective adhesion.

This primer is a watery, bituminous solution which can be applied with a brush; the solvent can be either white spirit (turpentine) or paraffin (kerosene). However, you must allow the primer to dry thoroughly before applying the flashing.

Once this is done, you simply cut a length of the self-adhesive flashing to more than adequately cover the damaged area and then press it into place. You may find that warming the flashing slightly, with a blowlamp, prior to application will make it easier to iron out the creases which sometimes occur.

For a repair using mastic, the area must again be thoroughly cleaned; only then can mastic be forced into the damage. Make sure that the mastic overlaps the crack by about 6mm, then lay a piece of roofing felt or aluminium foil over the top and press down. Once this is bedded, apply a further covering of mastic and brush a liquid bitumen proofing solution over the entire flashing and repair.

Mortar damage

Another way in which water can intrude beneath flashing is where it is turned, at its topmost edge, into the mortar between bricks. If the mortar joints are defective, even if the flashing itself is intact, there is nothing to stop water seeping into the roof space.

Use a cold chisel to remove all loose or suspect mortar, but ensure as you do so that the flashing remains held securely in the evacuated channel. If necessary, wedge the flashing in place with small pieces of wood. Then wet the joint and fill it with a mortar mix made up from four parts sand to one part of cement.

Replacing flashing

When severe pitting, holes and tears are evident, then the whole run of flashing will almost certainly need to be replaced. Methods for renewing flashing vary, both according to the types of material used and on the location on and around the roof. The task is not, however, as daunting as it might first appear.

Self-adhesive flashing can be used for complete replacement, though it is not as robust as the more traditional materials. First lever out the old flashing and wire-brush the whole area to get rid of loose mortar. Then cut the flashing to length, remove the backing paper and smooth it into place with a cloth and wooden seam roller. Take special care to check that the top edge of the flashing is in full contact with the brickwork—the slightest gap and water will seep in.

For a permanent repair, which should last a lifetime, lead and zinc can both be used. Lead is more pliable but zinc is cheaper, more available and weighs less.

Bending metals

With traditional materials you will have to master the art of bending in order to suit the shape and angle of the area to be covered.

Using either a chalk line or felt-tip marker, carefully measure and mark the point at which the metal is to be bent. Then lay the sheet of lead or zinc on your bench so that the mark is in line with the edge.

Next cramp a stout length of 75mm × 30mm batten over the work and line it up with the bending line. Use a board to force the overlap up or down, depending on the shape of the flashing. This will form a gentle bend which can then be consolidated with a hammer, bearing in mind that the metal is well protected by the timber.

Where you need an angle of more or less than 90°, a sliding bevel must be employed to transfer the angle at the site to your work. Constantly check the angle with the bevel until it is correct more or less along the entire length of the metal.

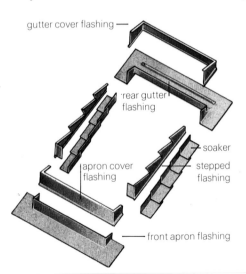

B. Semi-rigid mineral fibre sheet can be cut and folded to match all the components that go to make up a traditional sheet metal chimney flashing of the type shown here

gutter cover flashing
rear gutter flashing
soaker
apron cover flashing
stepped flashing
front apron flashing

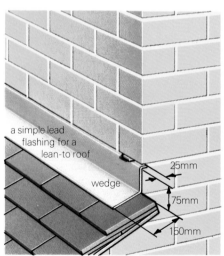

C. Straight flashings—in metal or mineral fibre—are formed on the bench. Once on the roof, they are mortared into the brickwork as shown, then dressed against the roof itself

a simple lead flashing for a lean-to roof
wedge
25mm
75mm
150mm

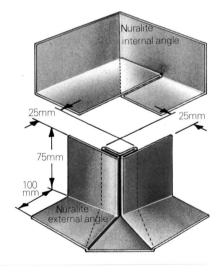

D. Internal and external corners are formed in semi-rigid mineral fibre sheet without cutting. The secret is to make central folds which expose or lose the excess as necessary

Nuralite internal angle
25mm
25mm
75mm
100mm
Nuralite external angle

1 *To mend an existing flashing using self-adhesive tape, apply the flashing primer first and then press the tape into position*

2 *Once you have bedded the length of tape in position, run a wallpaper seam roller or similar tool along all seams and edges*

3 *You can use self-adhesive flashing tape to make waterproof joints between walls and other types of roofing such as corrugated sheet*

4 *It is also ideal for jobs such as forming waterproof flashings where planted-on features such as porches and canopies are fitted*

5 *You can also use roofing felt and hot bitumen to form flashings. Apply the bitumen, re-heat it with a blowlamp and press on the felt*

6 *Complete a felt flashing of this sort by adding a capping layer and tucking its top edge into a chase cut in the wall above*

7 *You can solder small splits and tears in lead and zinc flashings so long as you use a high-powered soldering iron or blowlamp*

8 *If metal flashings are sound but have simply pulled out of their chases, wedge them back into place and re-mortar the chase*

9 *Once you have repaired splits and re-mortared chases, apply a coat of black bituminous paint to the flashing surface for extra protection*

10 To repair a damaged roof-ridge metal flashing with flashing tape, wire-brush the area and then clean it thoroughly with carborundum paper

11 Follow by painting on a coat of the special primer. Be sure to extend this well past the actual location of the damage

12 When the primer is touch dry, cut a suitable length of flashing tape, peel off the backing paper and press it firmly into place

13 Then iron out the crinkles and air bubbles by rolling over the tape with a hammer handle. Take extra care around the edges as you do this

14 To cut a length of Nuralite (semi-rigid mineral fibre sheet), score it with a handyman's knife and then snap it against a straightedge

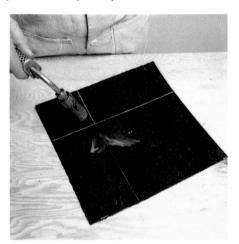

15 To make an internal corner, cut and mark out the Nuralite as shown then heat the whole area with a blowlamp until it is pliable

16 Use a wood block soaked with raw linseed oil and the straightedge to bend the softened Nuralite along the first of the folds

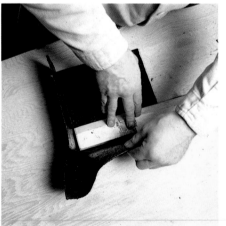

17 By the time you have finished, the sheet will be hard again— reheat it with the blowlamp before making the second fold

18 Once the basic creases are there, you can consolidate them with two oiled blocks. Press these hard into the folds and against each other

Fixing straight flashing

First lever out the old length of flashing and thoroughly rake out the mortar joints to a depth of 25mm.

Next, cut the replacement flashing to length and bend to fit in the manner described above. Remember that you will need to allow for a 19mm turnover strip along its entire length—this will be fed into the mortar joints and must be bent to an angle of 90°.

Wet the mortar joint and insert the turnover into it, wedging with small pieces of the metal you are using.

Now gently hammer the other angled section of the flashing to exactly match the downfall of the roof, taking great care not to accidentally break any tiles or slates. Finally fill the joint with mortar and clean the joint with a piece of rounded stick.

Replacing mortar flashing

Often, the flashing on a lean-to or garage wall is made up simply from mortar. This has a habit of cracking where it meets the vertical wall, so allowing water to penetrate. Non-hardening mastic can be used to repair small cracks but if the damage is severe, the whole length must be replaced with a proper flashing.

Remove the cement fillet and clean up the exposed brickwork and roof covering. Cut a slot 35mm deep in the abutting vertical wall, at least 75mm above (and parallel to) the adjoining roof. Note that the latter measurement will partially depend upon the location of a convenient mortar joint into which the slot can be cut. The apron—the part of the flashing which overlaps the roof—should be 150mm wide. So the width of the flashing strip should be 260–300mm.

19 *When you get to the corner, make the flap face outwards and press it together with the blocks. Add more heat if the sheet is too rigid*

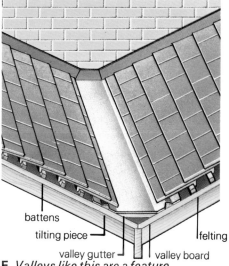

battens
tilting piece
valley gutter
valley board
felting

E. *Valleys like this are a feature of older properties. The metal linings are notoriously prone to deterioration and should be patched with flashing tape or semi-rigid asbestos*

The flashing is secured by forcing the 35mm turnover into the slot in the wall and wedging it in place with small, rolled pieces of the same metal. This slot is then filled with a 1:4 mortar mix.

If you are using lead, you will need to provide extra support with additional strips of metal called *tingles*. These are nailed into the rafters between the slates or tiles. Then, after the flashing is laid, they are bent over the front edge of the apron to stop it sliding down the roof.

Valley linings

Valley linings (fig. E) are a common feature of older properties—the very houses where damage due to ageing is likely to occur.

Small cracks and rents can be treated in much the same way as described for flashing, using either patches made up from self-adhesive flashing or a foil and mastic combination. Here, though, it is vital that the whole valley is treated with liquid bituminous proofing or a suitable liquid plastic coating.

Severe damage will inevitably mean total replacement and, as you will be removing a substantial number of tiles either side of the valley, ensure that you can quickly protect the exposed area from rain. Tarpaulin or heavy duty reinforced plastic sheet is ideal. You can replace the old lining with zinc or lead sheet, or even roofing felt, but probably the simplest cure is to use self-adhesive strip.

For the more traditional approach, you must first remove all the tiles

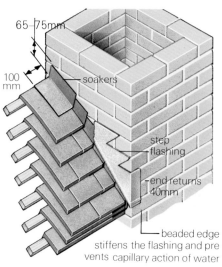

65–75mm
100 mm
soakers
step flashing
end returns 40mm
beaded edge stiffens the flashing and prevents capillary action of water

F. *The stepped soakers which form part of the flashings at chimneys and roof verges were traditionally cut from sheet metal; today you can buy them preformed in semi-rigid fibre*

covering both sides of the valley edge. Pull up the old lining and carefully lower it down to ground level. And while you are there, take the opportunity to check the state of the timber underlining; it is worthwhile treating it at this stage with a coat of preservative.

When you cut the new length of zinc or lead allow an overlap of about 50mm at the eaves. Place the new sheet over the underlining and work it into the shape of the valley, securing with galvanized nails.

Should you need to use more than one sheet, allow plenty of overlap between adjoining sheets to prevent water returning between them. You must also provide for a 75mm turning where the sheet meets the junction between wall and roof (fig. E).

Finish by securing the sheet to the battens on both sides working up from the eaves, and replacing the tiles in reverse number order. Use self-adhesive flashing along the length of the roof/wall junction to ensure effective waterproofing.

Flashing on a corner

Traditionally done with metal, flashing on a corner can be extremely difficult for the home handyman. The way to do it depends on the metal being used, but all methods demand a range of specialized tools and practical skills which are generally best left to a specialist.

One convenient material available for the do-it-yourselfer in the UK is semi-rigid mineral fibre sheet called Nuralite. This material is light in

20 Finish off the corner shaping using a wooden former made from two offcuts of blockboard

21 To make an external corner, mark a length as shown with one longitudinal line and five centre lines to indicate the four centre folds

22 Then, using the same heating-forming-heating process, fold the centre folds over one another to shorten the length by two folds

weight, waterproof and resistant to both abrasion and corrosion. It is easy to cut and, when heated with a blowtorch, can be bent and shaped. Nuralite also can be used as a roof covering and for making straight flashings in preference to lead or zinc figs B, D, F and 14 to 24).

Cutting: Straight cuts can be made by scoring deeply with a sharp knife and then breaking off the piece over the edge of a workbench or scaffold plank. Cut special shapes or irregular sections with a pair of tin-snips.

Bending: Use a crayon, pencil, or chalk line to mark the position of the bend. Place the line squarely over the edge of your bench and hold the sheet in position with a wooden batten cramped over the top.

Apply a blowtorch flame up and down the length of the area to be bent until the sheet begins to sweat and gradually bend of its own accord. As it does so, help form the shape slowly and firmly using a wooden block until you achieve the required angle. Both the block and the batten must be well sanded and kept lubricated with linseed oil or candlewax to prevent them sticking to the hot Nuralite.

For a bend of 90° turn over the sheet, align the angle point with the edge of the bench, reheat the sheet and press down the upstand with the wooden block until you achieve the right angle.

Joining: There are two methods used for joining this type of material—*delaminating* and *lap jointing*.

To delaminate Nuralite, heat the edge of one sheet, insert a knife blade into it and turn back about 25mm of the top layer of Nuralite. Next, melt

23 The folded length should now look like this. As before, consolidate the folds with oiled blocks and reheat if necessary

some bitumen No 1 welding block—available from larger builders' merchants—on to the inner surfaces and smooth it out using a paintscraper and heat from a blowtorch. Place the adjoining sheet between the two delaminated sections of the first and then heat them again with your blowtorch. Finally, consolidate the edges with a sealing or soldering iron.

For a lapped joint, both the surfaces to be joined must be well coated with No 3 bitumen compound (again available in block form). When working over small areas, heat the compound with a blowtorch and apply it directly to the sheets with a paint scraper. On larger surfaces, heat the bitumen block in a pot and then apply it with a suitable brush.

Heat the area to be coated and

24 Do the remaining corner shaping on the blockboard former, heating at intervals so that the centre folds splay out as shown

spread No 3 compound on both mating surfaces to a minimum width of 75mm. Bring the two together, apply more heat and flatten the entire area of the joint with a heated trowel.

Safety

When working at or above roof level always give thought to the safety of yourself and others. Use recognized scaffolding which is properly secured at ground level. Never leave tools or other heavy items unattended on the roof—they could slide off and hit someone. Try, whenever possible to work in company with someone else or at least make sure that help is close at hand if you need it.

UNDERSTANDING ELECTRICITY

Electric current explained ● Units of electrical measurement ● Loop, radial and ring-main circuits ● Earthing ● Fuses and circuit breakers ● Mending fuses ● Wiring a plug

Electricity in the home is something which we all take for granted—and would be lost without. Yet electricity is also highly dangerous if it is not treated with the respect it deserves. For the do-it-yourself enthusiast, this means having a sound knowledge of the way in which domestic installations work before tackling any electrical job with confidence.

Electricity and the law
In the UK, regulations covering wiring are compiled by the Institute of Electrical Engineers. Anyone may do

Above: *Electricity is very much taken for granted in homes today, because it is available at the flick of a switch*

their own wiring, but it is very sensible to follow the IEE regulations. These require that all electrical installations be tested on completion by the relevant electricity supply board.

Electrical measures
An electric current consists of a flow of minute particles called electrons. This flow can be likened to the flow of water from a tap connected by a pipe

to a storage tank.

For water to flow when the tap is opened, the tank must be at a higher level than the tap. And the greater the height of the tank, the higher the pressure of the water that comes out of the tap. So water at high pressure has a greater rate of flow, or current, than water at low pressure.

The *voltage* in an electrical circuit corresponds with the *pressure* of the water in the pipe. The *rate* of flow of an electric current is measured in *amperes* and is equivalent to the flow of water along the pipe—that is, how much comes out at any given time.

Electrical power is measured in *watts*. This term applies to the electrical equipment itself and is a measurement of the rate at which it uses electricity. An average electric light bulb uses only about 100 watts, whereas a powerful electric heater might use 3,000 watts (3 kilowatts). The relationship between amps, volts and watts is expressed in the formula:

$$\frac{\text{Watts}}{\text{Volts}} = \text{Amps}$$

This formula is useful for determining both the correct size of cable to use for an appliance and, in British systems, the correct size of cartridge fuse inserted in its plug.

Domestic installations
The comparison between the flow of water in a pipe and an electric current in a wire is not exact: electricity requires a closed loop—a circuit—in order to work.

Electricity comes into the home from a local transformer through an armoured service cable or via overhead wires. The service cable is connected to a fuse unit—called the company fuse—which is sealed by the electricity board or company. From here, power flows along the live supply wire and through the meter to the consumer unit—a

> **WARNING**
> In Australia and New Zealand, work on electrical installations must be approved by the supply authority and supervised by a licensed electrician.

combined fuse box and main switch, of which fig. E is one example. The live supply wire is usually encased in two separate sheaths. The electricity then flows through your lights and appliances before returning to the local transformer along the neutral wire. A third wire, the earth (properly known as the earth continuity conductor) links all parts of the circuit to the house's main earthing terminal.

Power circuits

The type of circuits found in British homes vary, depending on the age of the electrical installation. Lighting circuits are wired up on one of two systems, either the junction box or the loop-in; in either case the circuit cable leaves the fuse box and runs from lighting point to lighting point or junction box to junction box, terminating at the last light/box on the circuit.

Power circuits may be one of three types. In homes wired before about 1947, each socket outlet was supplied by its own circuit cable, running from the fuse box to the socket position (see B). Sockets were of three different sizes and current ratings—2, 5 and 15 amps—and took plugs with round pins. Such circuits were often dangerously over-extended and are now obsolete.

A: *Power runs to an appliance via the live wire and returns via the neutral. To safeguard against electric shocks, the switch is always on the 'live' side*
B: *For a wall switch, the live current must be diverted down the wall and back. Usually a standard two-wire cable is used, with wires of— confusingly—different colours. But both wires are in fact 'live'*

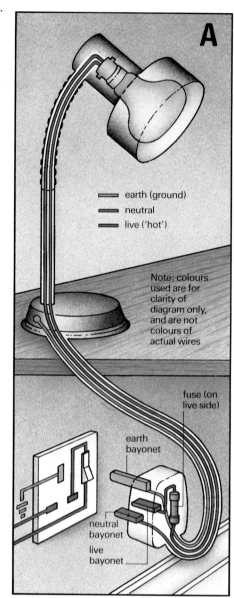

earth (ground)
neutral
live ('hot')

Note: colours used are for clarity of diagram only, and are not colours of actual wires

fuse (on live side)

earth bayonet

neutral bayonet

live bayonet

earth
neutral
live

These wires usually combined in one outer cable

Note: colours used are for clarity of diagram only, and are not colours of actual wires

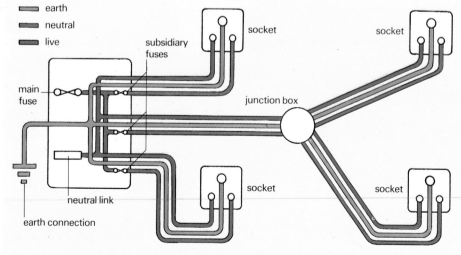

earth
neutral
live

main fuse

subsidiary fuses

socket

socket

junction box

neutral link

earth connection

socket

socket

Old radial circuit

C. *Radial circuit of the type used in homes before about 1947. The wire colours are the same as in newer wiring—red (live), black (neutral) and green (earth). Each socket is supplied by its own circuit cable, and the only fuse protection is at the fuse box. The sockets have round holes, and accept round-pin plugs, rated at 2, 5 or 15 amps according to size. Such circuits should be replaced immediately, since they may have been dangerously over-extended and are prone to overloading because of deterioration of the old rubber sheathing and insulation.*

Above: *Two-core-and-earth cable is used for most switch wiring. Since the black wire is technically live, it should be 'flagged' with red tape. The earth core links to the mounting box*

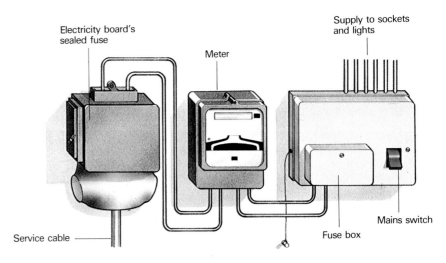

D. *Electricity enters the house through an armoured service cable connected to the company fuse. From here, power flows to the meter*

Below: *A modern consumer unit contains miniature circuit breakers instead of fuses, and possibly an earth leakage circuit breaker*

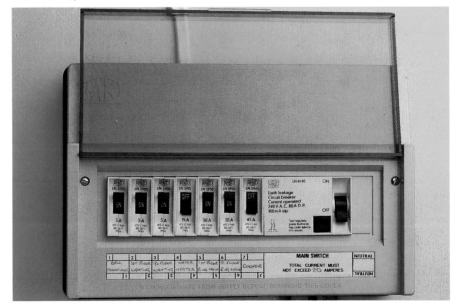

Ring-main system

In Britain, houses wired since 1947 use, for power socket circuits only, a different wiring system known as the *ring-main* circuit (fig. F). In this system, the live, neutral and earth wires run in a complete circle from the main switch to each socket in turn, and then back to the consumer unit. There is generally one ring for each floor of a house, with 'spurs' reaching out from it to supply isolated sockets.

Plugs and socket outlets in ring-main circuits are of the 13-amp rectangular pin type. These are much safer than the old round-pin types because the sockets have shutters inside which automatically close when a plug is withdrawn. Furthermore, ring-main plugs, unlike other types, carry their own cartridge fuses.

So if an individual appliance be-

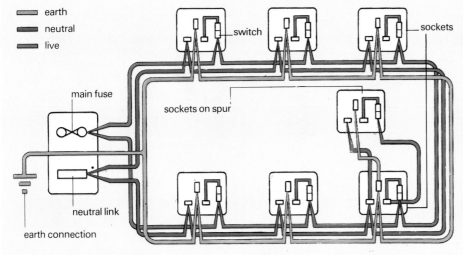

Ring-main

E. *The ring-main, exclusive to British houses. Each wire (the red 'live' for example) goes from the consumer unit to each socket in turn, and then back to the consumer unit, where the 'inward' and 'outward' ends are wired in together into the same hole in the appropriate terminal block. Each ring-main is protected by its own fuse in the consumer unit. In addition, each appliance that it serves has a fuse in the plug, lessening the chance of the main fuse blowing.*

comes faulty, only the fuse in its own plug—and not the main fuse for the whole circuit—will 'blow'.

Modern radials

Many modern wiring installations use a variation of the loop-in system already described for lighting circuits. Here the circuit cable runs from socket to socket, originating at the consumer unit and terminating at the last socket (see D). Modern radial circuits of this type may be wired up in two different ways depending on the floor area of the rooms they are serving—see Electrician 2, pages 7-10—but in each case the circuit may serve an unlimited number of sockets. Furthermore, spurs may be taken off the circuit to serve isolated sockets, as for ring-main extensions.

Modern radial circuits use the same 13-amp rectangular pin type of plug and socket as a ring-main. This means that, unlike old radial circuits, there are two levels of fuse protection—within the appliance plug itself, and also at the main consumer unit.

Earthing

Should a live wire come into contact with the metal casing of an appliance, anyone who touches the appliance is liable to receive a severe electric shock. For this reason, domestic appliances—apart from ones that are double insulated—have an earth wire connected to their outer casings and linked to the house earthing point.

This is so that, if a live wire makes contact with the casing, the electricity will follow the path of least resistance to earth; in other words, it will flow through the earth wire instead of the person's body. At the same time, a live wire coming into contact with earthed metalwork will result in a large current flow that also will blow the circuit or

plug fuse.

The electricity flows from the live wire in this way because it is trying to reach the neutral—which is connected to earth back at the electricity board transformer. This system has been found to be the safest way of disposing of unwanted current.

Fuses

A fuse is a deliberately weak link in the wiring, thinner than the wires on either side. If an overload occurs, the fuse wire melts and cuts off the current before the heat from the overload can damage equipment or cause a fire.

Fuses should always be of the nearest available size above the amperage of the appliance or circuit that they protect. Most electrical appliances have their wattage marked on a small plate fixed to the back or base of the unit. So, for an appliance connected to a ring-main, you can use the formula above to find the amp rating and hence the correct fuse to go in the appliance's plug.

For example, say an electric fire has a rating of 3 kilowatts and the voltage of the mains is 240 volts. The current taken by the fire is found by dividing the watts—3,000—by the volts—240—which gives a result of 12.5 amps. Therefore, the fire should be protected with a 13-amp fuse, the nearest higher size available.

In Britain, it is recommended practice to use 3-amp cartridge fuses, colour coded red, for all appliances rated up to 720 watts, and 13-amp fuses, colour coded brown, for everything else up to a maximum rating of 3 kilowatts—including TV sets, which take a high start-up current even though they are rated at below 720 watts, and so may blow a 3-amp fuse.

Above: *A residual current device (RCD) provides an additional level of safety by cutting the supply when it detects an earth current leak*

Residual current devices

Many modern wiring systems incorporate an additional safety measure called a residual current device (RCD)—formerly known as an earth leakage circuit breaker (ELCB). This detects current leaking to earth as a result of an electrical fault and shuts off the current in a fraction of a second if one occurs. This device may be fitted in a modern consumer unit (see page 103) or in a separate enclosure (as above).

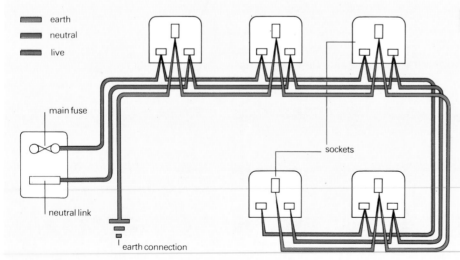

earth
neutral
live

main fuse

neutral link

earth connection

sockets

Modern radial circuit

F. *A modern radial circuit is wired like a loop-in lighting circuit, with the circuit cable running outwards from the consumer unit to each socket in turn, and terminating at the last socket on the circuit. It's a useful alternative to the ring main for adding circuits to extensions and conversions, or for reaching remote parts of the house where running a ring-main out and back would waste cable unnecessarily. The actual connections are made in exactly the same way as for a ring-main, and spurs may be taken off the circuit if required*

Mend a fuse

There are three main types of circuit fuse: wire fuses, cartridge fuses and circuit breakers. It is important to know which type you have and to keep a supply of spare fuse wire or cartridges. Circuit breakers need no spares as they are switches which automatically shut off if the circuit is overloaded at any time.

Most fuse boxes are covered by a plate which either clips on or screws into place. **Always turn off the mains switch before removing the plate or touching any fuse.**

With the plate removed you will see a row of fuse holders made of porcelain or moulded plastic (fig. G). Some are colour coded on the base: white for 5 amp lighting circuits, blue for 15 amp heating circuits, red for 30 amp power socket circuits and green for 45 amp cooker circuits. Alternatively, the amperage may be stamped on the front of the holder.

As a further guide it is a good idea to mark the fuse holders with the purpose of the circuit they protect— '1st floor sockets', 'Ground floor lights' and so on.

Take out the first fuse—the holders simply pull out and clip back into place—then replace the cover and turn the mains switch back on.

Check each circuit until you find the one that has stopped working. Turn off the mains again, remove the cover and mark the fuse holder accordingly. Afterwards, clip it back into place and repeat the operation for the other fuses in the box.

WARNING
In Australia and New Zealand, work on electrical installations must be approved by the supply authority and supervised by a licensed electrician.

When a fuse blows, the first thing to do is to discover the cause and rectify it. If you suspect that the failure is due to a faulty appliance, unplug it and do not use it again until it has been mended.

Sometimes fuses blow for no obvious reason. It may be that the fuse has just worn out in which case when it is replaced, the current will flow as before. But if a fuse keeps blowing each time it is replaced, there may well be a serious fault and you should contact an electrician.

Once the fault that caused the fuse to blow has been put right, locate the blown fuse. On *bridge wire* fuse holders (fig. G), the fuse wire is held in position by a screw at either end. The wire runs over the surface of the holder, so a broken fuse can be clearly seen. In *protected wire* fuse holders, the wire runs through a tube inside the holder. To check it, gently try to prise the wire out of the tube with a small screwdriver. If the fuse is blown, half of the wire will come away.

To mend a wire fuse, loosen the screws and discard the broken wire.

Replacement fuse wire is sold ready for use, mounted on a card. Use wire-cutters to cut a new length of wire of the correct amperage rating. Wrap the ends of the wire around the screws in a clockwise direction so that when you retighten the screws the wire is not dislodged. Finally, replace the holder and fuse box cover and switch the power back on.

In cartridge fuses, the wire is encased in the cartridge and can only be checked, at this stage, by replacement. Unclip the old cartridge and fit a replacement of the same amperage rating as the original.

When a circuit breaker shuts off, locate the fault that has caused it to do so, then reset the switch or button on the affected circuit.

When mending fuses, on no account be tempted to use a fuse of too high an amperage rating; you will be putting your entire electrical system—and possibly your life—at risk.

All the equipment you need for mending fuses—screwdriver, wire cutters and pliers—should be electrically insulated for maximum protection from electric shock.

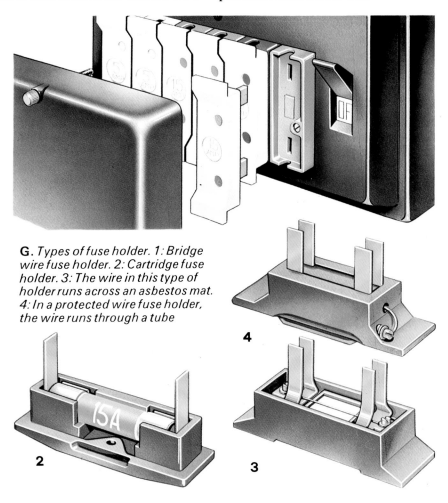

G. Types of fuse holder. 1: Bridge wire fuse holder. 2: Cartridge fuse holder. 3: The wire in this type of holder runs across an asbestos mat. 4: In a protected wire fuse holder, the wire runs through a tube

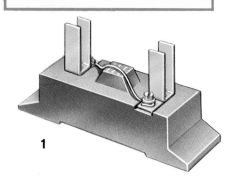

Wire a plug

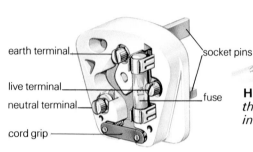

earth terminal

socket pins

live terminal

neutral terminal

fuse

cord grip

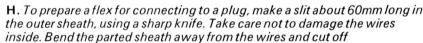

H. *To prepare a flex for connecting to a plug, make a slit about 60mm long in the outer sheath, using a sharp knife. Take care not to damage the wires inside. Bend the parted sheath away from the wires and cut off*

Cheap accessories invariably heat up in use—producing a fire risk—so it is important to use high quality plugs. Furthermore, it is essential to wire plugs correctly—incorrect wiring can be dangerous.

Remove the cover of the plug, by unscrewing the large screw between the pins, to reveal the three terminals which are attached to the pins of the plug. As you look at the plug, the terminal at the top connects to the green and yellow earth wire. The brown live wire connects via the fuse to the live pin on the right, and the blue neutral wire to the neutral terminal on the left.

Some older appliances have differently coloured wires; green for earth, red for live and black for neutral.

Appliances that are double insulated—such as television sets—do not have an earth wire so the earthing terminal should be left unconnected.

Loosen the cord grip which is secured by two screws at the base of the plug. The cord grip is to clamp the sheathing of the flex to the plug to prevent it from being pulled out accidentally. Some modern plugs are fitted with a fixed plastic gate in place of a conventional cord grip.

The sheathing of the flex must now be removed to a distance of about 60mm to allow the earthing wire to reach its terminal. Slit the outer sheath of the flex with a sharp knife taking care not to damage the wires (fig. H). Wires with damaged insulation should never be used.

Put the flex under the cord grip and firmly tighten the fixing screws so that the grip clamps the sheathing firmly in place. On plugs with a plastic gate, the sheathing should be pressed into position between the two halves of the gate.

Cut the three wires with wire clippers so that each can wrap round or pass through its terminal, then use a wire stripper to remove the insulation

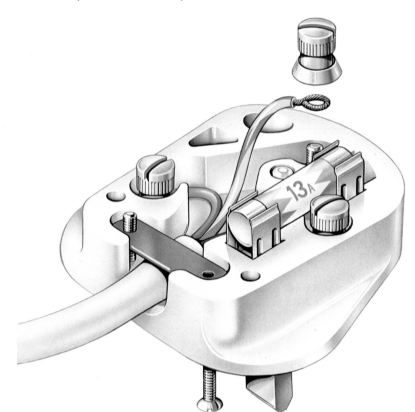

J. *Secure the flex in the cord grip by tightening its fixing screws. Strip the insulation from the end of the three wires, baring only enough wire to wrap safely around each terminal. Twist the strands and form a loop*

from the ends. Bare enough wire to fit around the terminal. Twist the strands making up each wire together then fasten the wires to their terminals making sure that there are no loose strands left free.

Remove the terminal nut and washer and form the wire into a closed, clockwise loop around the terminal so that it will not unravel it when the nut is being retightened (fig. J). Replace the washer and nut and tighten.

In some plugs, the wire passes through a hole and is secured by a small screw at the top of the terminal. Here, the wire should be bent double

before being inserted. Other, newer plugs have spring-loaded terminals: the flex core is simply pushed into the slot to be retained by the spring.

Finish off by clipping a working fuse into the fuseholder, making sure it is of the right amp rating for the appliance. Screw on the cover of the plug and it is ready for use.

Round pin plugs should be wired up in the same way as 13 amp plugs but, as they have no fuse, make sure that the current rating of the plug is adequate for the connected load.

When buying a plug, choose the type with sleeved pins; they prevent small fingers touching live metal at sockets.

OUTDOOR ELECTRICS

The uses of an outdoor supply ● Methods of installing a supply ● Overhead cables ● Underground cables ● Wall-mounted cables ● Types of armoured cable ● Making the connections ● Outdoor lighting ● Garden sockets

A. Below: *An electricity supply to an outhouse or garage – or even to a garden socket – can be very useful. Installation need not be difficult and the connections can be made according to normal practice providing you take special care to weatherproof them*

If you have a detached garage or greenhouse with no power supply, you will know how frustrating it can be to have to work occasionally in conditions of poor light and with a cobbled-up supply for your tools and appliances.

An electricity supply to a detached building – or even to a socket outlet in the garden – can be a boon if you intend to use an outhouse as a part-time workshop or if you use electrical garden tools. The installation work is not difficult; what is important is that you know how to make an outdoor supply safe.

Preliminary considerations
Unlike a lean-to garage or greenhouse, which you can supply off a ring main spur, detached buildings must have their own fused supply from the consumer unit.

The cables can be run in the normal way from the consumer unit to the point where they leave the house, and the same applies once they arrive at the outhouse. In between, however, you have a choice of three possible routes for the cables: overhead; underground; or along an outside wall (but not a fence).

An overhead cable must be fitted at a height of at least 3.5 (5.2m if there is access for vehicles underneath).

Underground cables must be buried in a trench at least 500mm deep and should be heavily protected – which applies also to cables run along a wall. Where the cable enters the house, drill a hole in the wall above the damp-proof course to accommodate it.

Materials
For overhead wiring you will need one or more lengths of 75mm sq treated timber to support the cable at the required height (allow at least a metre extra for posts that are to be sunk into

the ground). At the same time buy wall bolts to secure the posts, lengths of stout galvanized steel fencing wire to support them, and tensioning devices for the wire and a supply of twin core and earth PVC sheathed cable.

For underground cables you can use either armoured PVC insulated and sheathed cable, or PVC covered mineral insulated copper sheathed (MICS) cable, sold in the UK under the trade name 'Pyrotenax'. It is also possible to use ordinary PVC twin and earth cable if protected by high impact plastic conduit. Protect them by laying paving stones over the cable trench.

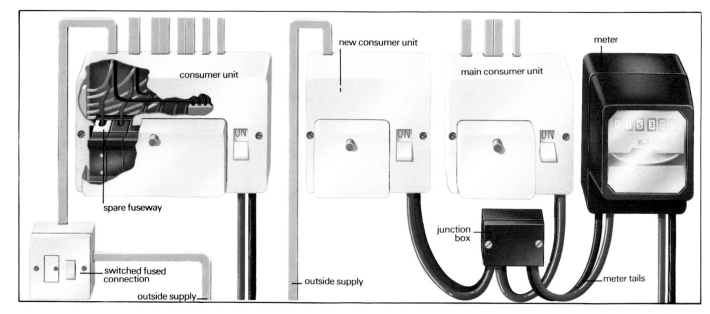

consumer unit

spare fuseway

switched fused connection

outside supply

new consumer unit

main consumer unit

outside supply

junction box

meter

meter tails

B. *Outdoor circuits need providing with special protection to prevent any possibility of electric shocks. So as well as a fuse or MCB (miniature circuit breaker) fit into the circuit a high-sensitivity residual current device or RCD (sometimes called a residual current circuit breaker, or RCCB). The switched fused connector (shown above) can carry the RCD (not shown). If you have a spare fuseway, add an extra consumer unit which the electricity board will connect via a junction box to their meter.*

To connect the armoured cables to the house and outbuilding circuits you will need special compression joints for connection to a steel junction box.
Size of cable: For a 20 amp supply over a distance greater than 20m, use 4mm² cable. You can also use 4mm² cable for 30 amp runs of less than 20m, but on longer runs you will need 6mm² cable to prevent excessive voltage drop.

Overhead cable installation
Drill a hole for the cable through an outside wall, so that the cable will lie beneath the upstairs floorboards. If that position does not give you enough height, go into the roof space and drill a hole through the wall above ceiling level or through the fascia board or soffit at the eaves.
Next feed the required length of cable through the hole and let it drop to the ground while you erect the post at the outbuilding end. Seal the hole with a non-hardening mastic. Mark off the end of the post which will be buried and then drill holes to take the

1 *When running a cable along an outside wall, use armoured cable of the correct size for its length and then fasten it with stout clips*

2 *Drill and plug holes in the brickwork for the clips and secure them with wood screws. Do not drill into mortar as this may cause it to crumble*

3 *Drill through house walls below the DPC, making sure you do not damage services inside the house. Use a long masonry bit for cavity walls*

4 *Allow enough length of cable for connection inside the house before feeding it through the wall and sealing the hole with non-hardening mastic*

expanding wall bolts.

Lower the post, drill the holes in the wall, and then screw an eye-bolt securely into the top of the post. Attach one end of the support wire to this, cut it to the correct length and then securely fix a wire tensioner to the other end.

The support wire must be bonded to earth for safety reasons. Connect one end of a length of 2.5mm² green and yellow PVC insulated cable to the eye-bolt and clip this to the post using cable clips. Allow enough length for the cable to be attached to the switched fused connection unit.

Next run the power cable from the house to the outbuilding and lay it alongside the support wire. Allow enough extra length to reach the inside of the building from the top of the post and then clip it to the support wire using stout cable ties every 1m or so. Raise the post again, fit it into its hole and bolt it to the wall. Fill in the hole

and compact the earth around the post as hard as you can by stamping on it.

Returning to the house, get up on a ladder and drill and plug a hole in the wall or the eaves for another eye-bolt as close as possible to the cable entry point. Screw in the eye and then pull the free end of the cable support wire up to it. Fix the wire securely and take up the slack with the tensioning device. Inside the house take up the slack on the cable and either run the wire directly back to the consumer unit or cut it off close to the entry point and leave about 3m inside the house for connection.

Underground cables
Decide first where the cable will enter the house – you will have to drill a hole for the cable through one of the walls above the DPC or through a corner of an air brick. If you cannot do this without going through

the wall above the floorboards, or if you have a solid floor, choose a room where the sight of exposed cable does not matter too much – a laundry room is ideal.

Once you have finalized the route of the trench, mark it out with string and pegs and start digging. The trench should be 500mm deep and about 300mm wide. When you have finished, remove any flints or sharp stones from the base and cover it with a 50mm layer of fine sand or sifted soil to act as a cushion.

Armoured cable can be laid directly into the trench, but if you are using PVC sheathed cable and conduit assemble the conduit first to make sure it fits before dismantling it again and threading the cable through. Allow about 1m of cable inside each building for connection.

Secure the conduit or cable to the walls with saddle fasteners and lay slabs of concrete over the cable in the trench to protect it from spades and forks at a later date. Fill in the trench compacting the earth as you do so.

Outside walls
Where the cable can be run along the outside wall of the house or along a garden wall, use the same cable types as for underground installations. Pass the cable through the house wall in the same way as for underground or overhead installations, depending on how high off the ground you intend to route it. Secure the cable to the walls using saddle fasteners.

Supply and connections
Once you have installed the outside cables, you can lay the supply cables inside the house. If you have a spare fuseway inside the consumer unit, use this for the supply to the outbuilding. If not, ask the electricity board to cut off the power and connect a supply from the meter to a new consumer unit once you have completed the rest of the installation.

Start by screwing a fixed appliance outlet or new consumer unit to the wall next to the consumer unit – this will allow you to isolate the entire cable and out-building circuit without having to fiddle with the fuses in the unit (fig. B).

Connect to the outlet a length of twin and earth cable of the same cross-sectional area as the cable outside. Run the outer end of the cable to the consumer unit and leave it there. Now run more of the same cable from the switched fuse connection unit to the outside cable entry point – follow normal wiring practice in routing and fixing it.

If the outside cable is twin and earth PVC sheathed, connect the two using a junction box screwed to the inside wall, to a floor joist below the floorboards, or to a ceiling joist in the roof space. If the outside

5 *Remove any turf on the route of an underground cable before digging a trench 500mm deep and about 300mm wide in which to bury it*

6 *Unroll the cable into the trench, making sure that it is not kinked. For a garden socket, allow 1m of cable at the end of the trench for connection*

7 *Cover the cable with fine sand or soil before laying slabs of concrete or concrete cable tiles to protect it from garden spades and forks*

8 *Prepare Pyrotenax for connection by stripping off the outer PVC sheathing for about 150mm and slipping the rubber boot over the end*

cable is MICS or armoured, cut it off inside the house at a suitable mounting point for a junction box. Screw a steel knockout switch box directly to the inside wall or a joist at this point and remove a knockout on two opposite sides.

Prepare the outside cable by stripping off about 150mm of the outer PVC and armoured sheathing to expose the wires. The compression fittings which join the cable to the switch box are exactly the same as those for copper pipe and are fitted in the same way. Slip the capnut over the PVC sheathing and then fit and tighten the threaded gland. Insert the fitting into one of the holes in the box and secure it with a back nut. Fit a PVC grommet over the other hole in the box, slip the PVC sheathed cable through and connect the two cables using a three-way terminal block. Use a blanking plate to seal the box.

Repeat the connection procedure at the outbuilding end then run twin and earth cable of the correct cross-sectional area to a switched fused connection unit mounted on the wall near the door. From here, run the cable to the lights, switches, and socket outlets in the building.

Outside lighting

Outside lighting takes many forms, ranging from floodlights mounted on the house walls, or concealed in the garden, to courtesy lights mounted at the end of the drive on the gate posts. A wide range of weatherproof lights is available, most of which operate on mains voltage. Some – taking bulbs similar to car head-lamp units – operate at a lower voltage and require a transformer.

Power supplies to outside lights are run

9 *Slip the compression fittings over the end of the exposed copper sheathing and slide them well down the cable out of the way*

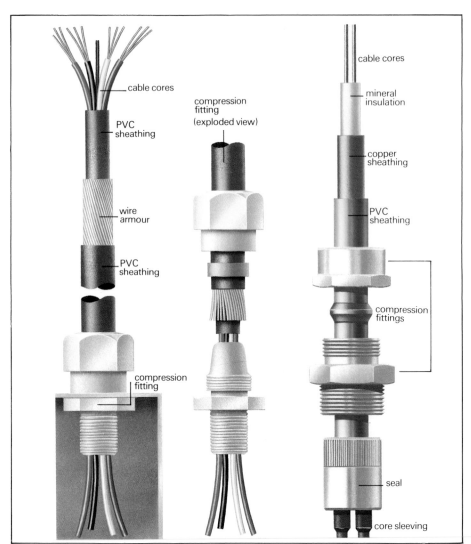

C. *The two main types of armoured cable: PVC sheathed wire-armoured cable (left and centre) shown with its compression fittings exploded and fitted*

to a switch box. Pyrotenax armoured cable (right) is shown with its slightly different compression fittings and watertight seals in place

Labels in figure C:
- cable cores
- PVC sheathing
- wire armour
- PVC sheathing
- compression fitting
- compression fitting (exploded view)
- cable cores
- mineral insulation
- copper sheathing
- PVC sheathing
- compression fittings
- seal
- core sleeving

10 *Now strip back about 70mm of the copper sheathing. As you do this the mineral insulation will crumble away to expose the cable cores*

11 *Screw the pot on to the exposed copper sheathing using a pair of pliers – making sure that it goes on absolutely straight*

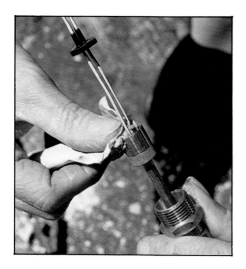

12 *Slip the watertight seal over the ends of the cores and then press sealing compound firmly into the pot to separate them*

13 *Press the seal down hard to compress the compound and then slip sleeving over the cores, leaving about 20mm exposed for connection*

14 *Mark one of the cores with a piece of red tape to identify it as the live wire and use a meter or test bulb to identify the other end*

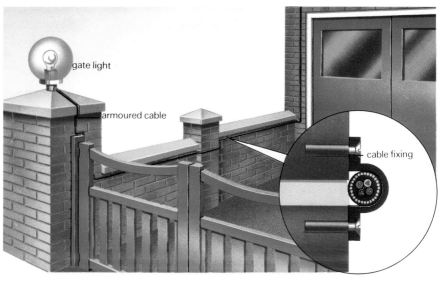

gate light

armoured cable

cable fixing

15 *Attach Pyrotenax to a switch or junction box by slipping the compression gland into a knockout hole and securing it with a back nut*

in exactly the same way – and using the same materials – as the supply to an outbuilding. The only exception is where a light is fixed directly to the outside wall of the house: here you can supply the unit through a hole drilled in the wall with the switch inside the house.

Gate lights can be supplied with either an underground or a wall-mounted cable, MICS and armoured cable being run directly to the light fitting itself. If you wish to install an outside switch as well, use a weatherproof lockable key switch to prevent tampering by vandals and children. These are fitted and connected in exactly the same way as their domestic counterparts indoors.

Transformers should ideally be located inside the house or an outbuilding but many are weatherproof and can be located discreetly in the garden. Make sure, however, that all the cable entry points are protected by weatherproof seals.

D. Above: *An outside gate light with a wall-mounted power supply. This kind of supply can be used for other types of light and also for garden sockets*

Fairy lights: There are a number of units ideal for fairy lights. These have two steel pins projecting from the lampholder which are protected by a weatherproof screw-on cover and are called Festoon lampholders (fig. E).

To connect the lampholders run a twin and earth 4mm² seven-strand cable from a 13 amp socket in the house or the garden (see below) and lay it out on a lawn or similar flat surface. Unscrew the cover on the pins, press the cable on to them so that one pin pierces each core, and screw the cap firmly back in place.

Use a maximum of 10 lampholders per circuit with a bulb rating of 40 watts. The last lampholder on the circuit should conceal the cut end of the cable.

When you hang the lights – whether in a tree or from a support wire slung between two poles, trees or buildings – make sure that the cables are not under tension and that the bulbs cannot get blown against branches or walls; if this happens, the bulb may break and expose the filaments which could be dangerous in wet weather.

Once you have made up a set of fairy lights in this way, do not remove any of the lampholders or you will expose holes in the wire which, in wet weather, could cause a short circuit.

Garden socket outlets

Because so many garden tools are now electrically powered, a socket outlet in the garden can be very useful. And if your garden is quite small you may be able to fit the socket on the outside wall of the house or outbuilding.

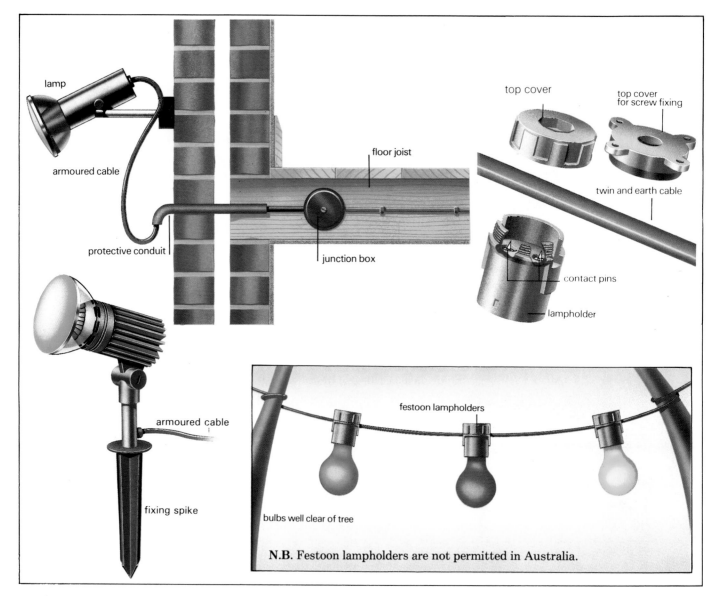

lamp

armoured cable

protective conduit

floor joist

junction box

top cover

top cover for screw fixing

twin and earth cable

contact pins

lampholder

armoured cable

fixing spike

festoon lampholders

bulbs well clear of tree

N.B. Festoon lampholders are not permitted in Australia.

E. *Clockwise from top left: wall-mounted spotlight; festoon lampholder; fairy lights between trees; garden spotlight*

Buy either a heavy duty weatherproof unit or use a standard surface-mounted socket with a proprietary weatherproof plastic cover. Make sure, however, that the cable entry and the pin holes are protected with a weatherproof seal.

The supply for an outside socket can be taken from a ring main spur, if it is mounted on the outside wall of the house; otherwise a separate circuit is needed. Run the cable inside the house to the socket position and drill a hole in the outside wall at the socket height. Remove one of the knockouts in the back of the mounting box, feed the cable through the wall and the box to the socket plate, and screw the box down so that it conceals the hole in the wall. Seal the joint between the box and the wall with

mastic, connect up the socket and screw the plate to the box.

A socket in the garden itself should be screwed to a treated timber post securely sunk into the ground. The socket should be high enough off the ground to prevent inadvertent damage from lawn mowers and boots while you are working.

Supply the socket through an underground armoured or MICS cable that connects directly with a spare fuseway at the consumer unit.

Extension leads: These are extremely useful for temporary outside work, but they must not be used as a permanent supply to an outbuilding or power tool, and they should not be used in wet weather in any circumstances.

Always disconnect the extension lead (at the mains end) when you are not using it, as a spade or rake could pierce the sheathing and cause a serious and possibly fatal shock.

Fountain pumps

There are several designs for these on the market—some are intended for total immersion in a garden pond and others for use alongside it. As the majority are 12 or 24 volt units you will need to use a transformer to supply them (see above).

Read any wiring instructions carefully—especially those concerning safety. There should be no way in which water can reach and short-circuit any of the electrical connections.

Cables from the transformer to the pump should be run underground in plastic conduit and then looped over the edge of the pool—for a submersible pump—where it can be hidden by rocks and pond plants. Pumps by the side of the pool can have the power supply coming from directly underneath them so that there is no exposed wiring at all. Plumb them in to the pond following the manufacturer's instructions.

INSTALLING FIXED APPLIANCES

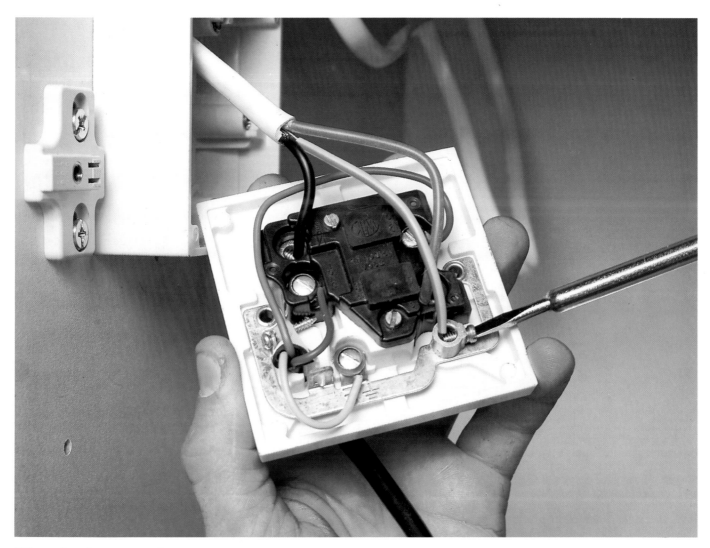

Fixed electrical appliances are sometimes best connected to the mains supply, not through a plug and socket, but through a fixed outlet

A fixed outlet, unlike a normal socket outlet, does not accept a plug. Instead, the flexible cable from an electrical appliance is wired directly to terminals within the outlet. This increases safety, because without unscrewing the outlet, there is no possibility of anyone touching live terminals. Fixed outlets are widely used in UK wiring for fixed room heaters, immersion heaters, freezers, washing machines and so on.

The circuit to supply these appliances can either be run from a spare fuseway or be in the form of a spur branching off a ring main.

The fixed outlet—the point where

> **WARNING:** Always make sure that the electricity is turned off before starting work. If you have rewirable fuses, turn off the main switch and remove the appropriate circuit fuse before restoring power to the rest of the house. If you have miniature circuit breakers, simply switch off the relevant one.

you connect the appliance—can be a fused connection unit, a double-pole switch, or a cord outlet unit. The maximum loading for any one of these outlets is 3000 watts.

1 *The most convenient place to take a spur from is a socket outlet. To start with, isolate the supply, and remove the socket cover*

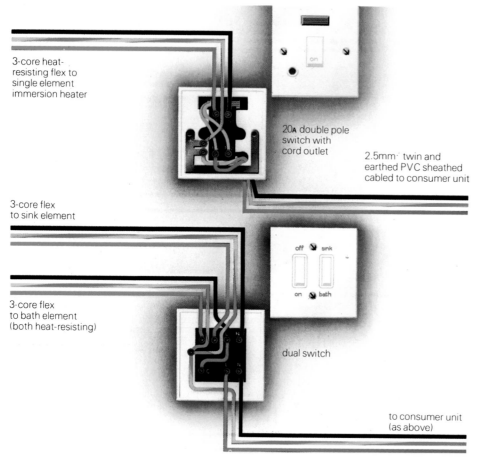

3-core heat-resisting flex to single element immersion heater

20A double pole switch with cord outlet

2.5mm² twin and earthed PVC sheathed cabled to consumer unit

3-core flex to sink element

3-core flex to bath element (both heat-resisting)

dual switch

to consumer unit (as above)

A. Left: *A 20A double-pole switch used in an immersion heater circuit. Switched outlets must be positioned outside a bathroom*
Below left: *A special dual switch used in a twin element immersion heater circuit*

Because of this, it is only safe to supply something as powerful as an immersion heater from a ring circuit spur if the circuit is lightly loaded—such as one supplying the upstairs part of the house only.

But for other, less demanding, appliances, taking the supply from a ring circuit spur is the ideal solution as long as the number of unfused spurs from the circuit does not exceed the number of socket outlets already present.

Where an appliance is supplied from a ring circuit spur, it is essential that a fuse—the equivalent of the fuse in a 13 amp plug—be inserted somewhere in the spur circuit. Without this, the only protection the circuit would have is the 30 amp fuse in the consumer unit which requires up to 60 amps to blow it if it's the rewirable type.

Direct from the consumer unit

If you have a spare fuseway in your consumer unit, taking an exclusive circuit from here is usually a simple job—and in the case of an immersion heater, almost essential.

Where there are no spare fuseways, you can either replace the consumer unit with one containing more fuseways—a rather expensive solution—or install a *switchfuse* unit which is, in effect, a small consumer unit containing one or two fuses.

Ring circuit spurs

Though ring circuit spurs can be used to supply any of the above mentioned appliances, you must be careful not to overload the ring circuit. For example, while an extractor fan takes about 40 watts and a heat/light unit about 700 watts, an immersion heater takes 3000 watts and is better run on a separate radial circuit.

In the UK, the maximum load capacity of a ring circuit is 7200 watts; but for safety reasons it is wise not to exceed a loading of 6500 watts. So if you supply an immersion heater—which is classed as a continuous load—from a ring circuit, you immediately take up half the recommended loading.

2 *Disconnect the socket and extend the cables using connector blocks Use 2.5mm² twin core and earth, PVC sheathed cable*

3 *If you do not wish to channel the cables in the wall, take the extended cables into a wall-mounted pattress, over the existing socket*

4 *Take a switched fused connection unit, and nibble away an opening in the rear of the pattress to run the cable from the socket outlet*

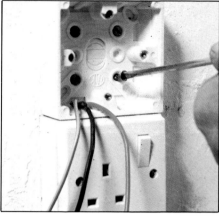

5 *Connect the extended cables up to the socket back, then connect another set of cables to the socket and run them up to the connector*

6 *Mark the position of the pattress on the wall, directly above the socket, then drill the holes, plug the wall and fix the pattress in place*

7 *Strip about 9mm of insulation off each of the cables and then connect them up to the appropriate terminals on the connection unit*

Fixed outlets

As mentioned above, you have a choice of three types of fixed outlet.

Fused connection unit: This is quite simply a terminal box and fuse carrier containing a small cartridge fuse. It is housed in a square, one-gang cover plate (faceplate) for mounting in a standard, one-gang plastics or metal box. The fuses are identical to those fitted in 13 amp fused plugs.

In the UK, they are stamped BS.1362 and the 13 amp is brown, the 10 amp black, the 5 amp black, the 3 amp red and the 2 amp black. When buying these fuses, take great care to purchase the right ones: slightly smaller ones are available which are marked BS.646, and are intended for use in dimmer switches, shaver socket outlets and the like, not in fused connection units.

Fused connection units come in two forms—switched and non-switched—and have a flex outlet attached and/or a neon indicator.

Double-pole switch: This is a rocker switch on a standard, square one-gang faceplate for mounting in a standard 1-gang plastic or metal box. Used as the mains outlet for a fixed appliance, it has a 20 amp current rating.

Like fused units, double-pole switches come in a variety of styles—

with and without a neon indicator and with and without a flex outlet—but because they contain no fuses, you must fit one of the appropriate current rating somewhere in the circuit.

Flex outlet unit: Also known as a cord outlet, this is a square, one-gang standard faceplate with a hole in the centre through which a circular, sheathed flex can pass. At the back of the plate is a three-way terminal block and a flex, or cord, clamp. The function of the unit is to connect the flex which feeds the appliance to the fixed circuit wiring. In fact it is used in much the same way as a ceiling rose in a lighting circuit.

A flex outlet is generally used as the mains outlet to a fixed appliance where no other outlet may be used, such as in a bathroom where a low-mounted wall heater needs to be controlled by a remote, cord-operated, ceiling switch.

Connecting a fixed spur

Where a ring circuit spur is to supply a fixed appliance, the spur cable should be connected to the ring main at a convenient point. Typically this will be either at the terminals of an existing ring socket outlet, or at a 30 amp three-terminal joint box inserted into the ring cable at a con-

venient place, such as under the floorboards.

For many appliances—such as wall heaters, waste disposers and central heating electrics—the necessary fuse for the spur can be that in the fused connection unit fixed near the appliance and connected to it by flexible cord or cable.

The spur cable from the point where it joins the ring circuit to the fused connection unit must be 2.5mm². The size of the flex from the connection unit will be smaller and must be suited to the connection unit fuse—itself determined by the type of appliance.

Where the outlet unit is to be a double-pole switch or a flex outlet, the necessary fuse should be situated away from the appliance. The best position is at, or near, the point where the spur cable is connected to the ring cable and will take the form of a non-switched, fused connection unit. This can be fixed next to the ring socket outlet to which the spur is connected.

Where the spur is supplied from a joint box, you run a 2.5mm² cable from the joint box to the non-switched

B. Below: *Connect up a 2.5mm² spur from a ring circuit cable by cutting in a three-terminal junction box*

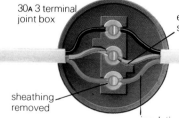

ring cable

30A 3 terminal joint box

earth cut and sheathed

sheathing removed

insulation stripped but wire not cut

ring cable

spur cable

8 *Next secure the surface mounted cable channel to the wall, either with contact adhesive on a smooth wall or with screws if it is uneven*

9 *Now run the 2.5mm² spur cable from the appliance fixed outlet through the channel to the spur fuse connector, and connect it up*

10 *Finally secure the cable channel cover in place, and replace the front panel of the switched fuse connector spur*

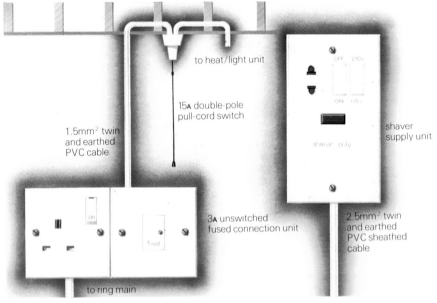

to heat/light unit

15A double-pole pull-cord switch

1.5mm² twin and earthed PVC cable

shaver supply unit

3A unswitched fused connection unit

2.5mm² twin and earthed PVC sheathed cable

to ring main

C. Above: *The outlets in a bathroom for a heat/light unit and a shaver supply unit. In the former, connection must be outside the bathroom; the shaver unit has an isolating transformer*

fused connection unit situated on the wall above the skirting board. And since the spur cable running from a fused connection unit is protected by the unit's own fuse, a lighter weight cable can be used to connect it to the appliance. Normally this will be 1.5mm² twin and earth PVC sheathed cable, which has a current rating of 13 amps. No other fuse is required in the spur circuit.

Installing an immersion heater

To wire an immersion heater on an exclusive circuit you need a length of 2.5mm² twin core and earth PVC sheathed cable, a control switch, a length of heat-resisting cable or flex and a 15/20 amp fuseway in your consumer unit. Providing a spare fuseway exists, all you need do is replace the blanking plate with a 15 amp fuse carrier and fuse.

Although there may not appear to be a spare fuseway, it is often possible to create one by rearranging the circuits. For example, a bell transformer and a couple of lights may be on separate circuits, even though they can quite easily share the same circuit. But if you do create a spare fuseway in this manner, do not forget to exchange the the 5 amp fuse on the old circuit for one which has the necessary 15 amp current rating.

The next step is to run the twin and earth PVC-sheathed cable from the 15 amp fuseway to where the immer-

sion heater control switch is to be located on the wall.

For a single-element immersion heater, or a twin element immersion heater with a change-over switch on the heater head, the control switch to use is a 20 amp double-pole switch with cord outlet and—preferably—a neon indicator. Here, the circuit wires are connected to the mains or supply terminals of the switch and the heat-resisting flex to the load terminals.

For a twin-element immersion heater of the type which requires a change-over switch for selection of either element, use a two-in-one switch— also known as a dual switch—which consists of the necessary double-pole switch and a change-over switch on one faceplate. Typically these will be marked on/off and sink/bath respectively. A dual switch is also used where you have two separate immersion heaters fitted to one cylinder.

As the circuit fuse in the consumer unit is of the appropriate rating for both the circuit and the heater, no separate fuse unit is required.

Heat/light units

Heat/light units are often used in bathrooms in place of the standard light fitting. But although the unit might replace a light, it must never be connected to the lighting circuit. Instead it must be on a separate circuit, such as a ring circuit spur.

Although heat/light units typically have cord-operated switches for the light and heater, in the UK an independent switch is also required; and in the bathroom, this must also be of the cord-operated, ceiling-mounted type.

The circuit for a heat/light unit can be a fused spur with a non-switched

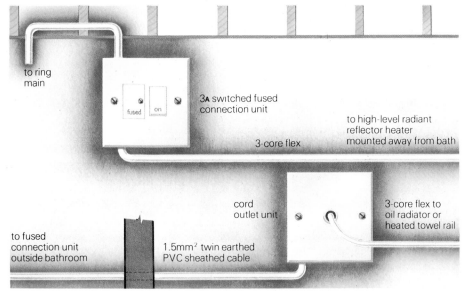

to ring main

3A switched fused connection unit

to high-level radiant reflector heater mounted away from bath

3-core flex

cord outlet unit

3-core flex to oil radiator or heated towel rail

to fused connection unit outside bathroom

1.5mm² twin earthed PVC sheathed cable

D. Left: *The outlets for two different types of bathroom heater. The upper example must be mounted out of reach, and the heater is operated by means of its own cord-operated switch*

fused connection unit situated where the spur connects with the ring cable outside the bathroom.

Shaver socket

A shaver socket installed in the bathroom is correctly termed a shaver supply unit. In the UK, it is rated at the standard 240 volts, but contains a double-wound transformer to isolate both socket and shaver from the earthed mains electricity.

Owing to the stringent design specifications in force the unit can be supplied direct from a ring circuit spur, using 2.5mm² twin and earth cable with no intervening fuse: a thermal cut-out prevents any other portable appliance—even a portable lamp—from being supplied by it. Shaver sockets in rooms other than the bathroom often have no transformer and are supplied from the lighting circuit.

Wall heaters

The term wall heater covers a wide range of heaters including radiant reflector heaters (formerly termed infra-red heaters), oil-filled radiators, panel heaters and skirting heaters.

Radiant reflector heaters: A typical radiant reflector heater has one or more spiral wire elements enclosed in silicon quartz tubes, and produces a directional flow of radiant heat. They are usually located high up when used in the bathroom or a child's bedroom.

As these heaters have open elements, although protected by a mesh guard, UK regulations require that they must be supplied through a double-pole switch fixed within reach. The appropriate fixed outlet is therefore a switched fused connection unit with a flex outlet.

The switch of all fused connection units is double-pole; a switched socket outlet usually has a single-pole switch, complete isolation being obtained by pulling out the plug.

In the bathroom, a wall-mounted radiant reflector heater should be fixed at high level and on the opposite wall to the bath. The switched fused connection unit can be fixed at the side of the heater and connected to it by circular sheathed flexible cord. The heater must be switched on and off by its own cord-operated switch, the switch of the fused connection unit being used only to isolate the heater from the mains when necessary.

The fused connection unit can be supplied direct from a ring circuit spur using 2.5mm² twin and earth PVC sheathed cable.

Low-mounted wall heaters: The electrical outlet for low-mounted wall

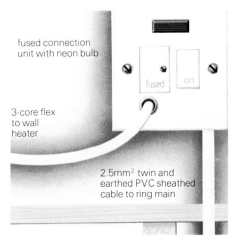

fused connection unit with neon bulb

3-core flex to wall heater

2.5mm² twin and earthed PVC sheathed cable to ring main

E. *This is a switched fused connection unit with a neon indicator and a front flex outlet*

heaters—such as oil filled radiators—can be either a 13 amp socket outlet (except in the bathroom), or a switched fused connection unit. The outlet is fixed at the flex or terminal box end of the heater and should ideally be mounted on the wall above the skirting board—about 300mm above floor level.

Generally, the socket outlet or fused connection unit will be supplied from a ring circuit spur; but as this type of heater is usually situated along the route of a ring circuit, it can be connected to the ring cable itself. The ring cable can be looped in and out of the socket or run to a connection unit in the usual manner.

Where a low-mounted heater or a heated towel rail is fixed in the bathroom, a different outlet is required. In the UK, socket outlets are prohibited in a bathroom and any switch must be out of reach of the bath. So, instead, use a flex outlet supplied from a fused spur. If necessary, a cord-operated switch can also be fitted near the appliance in the bathroom.

Sink and basin water heaters

Electric storage water heaters of 10 litre capacity and instantaneous water heaters each have a current loading of 300 watts and so can be supplied from ring circuit spurs. The mains outlet can be either a switched fused connection unit or a socket outlet, preferably the former.

Where the wash basin is in the bathroom, the fused connection unit should be mounted at a high level so that it is out of reach of anyone using the bath or shower. Instead of flexible cord, twin and earth PVC sheathed cable—fixed to, or buried in, the wall—should be run from the connection unit to the heater. An alternative is to have a cord-operated switch and a flex outlet supplied from a fused spur.

Extractor fan

An extractor fan can be supplied either from a ring circuit spur or from the lighting circuit, whichever is the more convenient. With either supply, the circuit connection is best made in the ceiling space above the fan.

The ring circuit spur cable can terminate at either a switched/fused connection unit situated near the fan or a fused clock connector. The latter has a removable 'plug' to which the flex is connected and contains a fuse of either 3 amp or 1 amp rating. Removing the 'plug' isolates the fan from the mains electricity.

When a fan is supplied from a lighting circuit, no fuse is needed but a clock connector is still the best accessory for connecting the fan flex to the fixed circuit wiring. Where the extractor fan does not contain a cord-operated switch, or where a reversing facility is needed, a control switch can be fixed at a lower level and the circuit wiring run to the controller first.

Waste disposer
A waste disposer requires a switched fused connection unit, ideally supplied from a ring circuit spur. With many models of waste disposer the control

F. Below: *The various circuits for fixed appliances in the kitchen. All the appliances require a fused spur. Note how the extractor fan circuit on the left is fused, properly, before the control unit. (Left to right) The circuits are for an extractor fan, a water heater, a waste disposal unit, and a central heating boiler. In all cases you must use a 2.5mm² cable from the ring circuit*

unit—which sometimes includes a reversing control—is mounted on the disposer body. The flex from the fused connection unit should run direct to this controller and be connected to the mains terminals. Where the controller is a separate unit, it can be mounted next to the fused connection unit.

As this is a low-level mains outlet, it is best—where possible—to run the spur cable up from below the kitchen floor where it can be connected to a 30 amp joint box inserted into the ring cable. If you have a solid floor, run the spur from a socket outlet situated above the work surfaces.

Central heating outlet
The mains outlet for a central heating pump and controls usually presents the same problems as a waste disposer outlet as this, too, is fixed at a low level. It is best located on the wall as near as possible to the pump or controller mains terminals. The outlet should be a switched fused connection unit with a flex outlet. Alternatively, you could use a 13 amp socket outlet, though there is always the chance that the plug will be accidentally withdrawn to enable another appliance to be used, and not be replaced immediately.

· The sheathed flexible cord should be

of the heat-resisting type. With some installations, cable—rather than flex—is used for the connection. If so, the fused connection unit should not have a flex outlet. Although not essential, it is useful to have a plate with a neon indicator.

Before wiring the circuit and fixing the mains outlet, you should consult the manufacturer's instructions provided with the boiler, pump and controls: the electrical requirements differ between different installations.

Kitchen electrical appliances
Most electrical appliances used in the kitchen are completely portable and are plugged into socket outlets, but for those which are fixed, a supply taken from a switched fused connection unit is most convenient. Washing machines, dishwashers, freezers and refrigerators with a loading of not more than 3000 watts can all be supplied from 13 amp mains outlets. Conventional electric cookers have much higher loadings and require 30 or 45 amp circuits. This will be covered later in the course.

The fused connection units for fixed appliances can either be supplied from ring circuit spurs or wired into the ring cable of the circuit as they are installed.

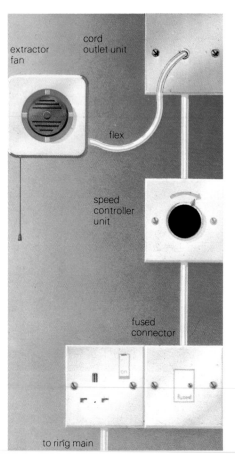

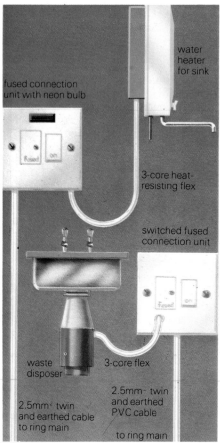

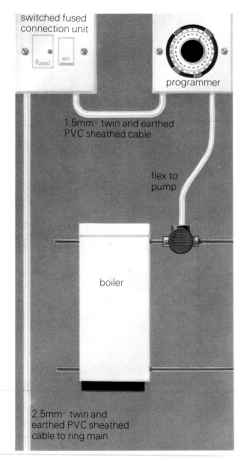

INSTALLING A PORCH LIGHT

A porch light does more than light the way to your front door: it also acts as a powerful deterrent to prowlers. Fitting one as an extension to your house lighting is a simple job.

A porch light is good way to brighten up your home—it says 'welcome' to the guests you want, and it helps deter the prowlers you'd rather not have around. And by lighting the way to your front door, it can help prevent accidents on dark nights.

Types of fitting

Most 'porch' lights are not actually fitted inside a porch—if the porch is fully enclosed and weatherproof you could fit an ordinary light fitting in it—but are usually fitted just outside the front or back door, often on the house wall. They can also be hung from the roof of open porch canopies.

Although there are hundreds of different porch lights on the market, they fall into about half a dozen broad categories. The basic types are:

carriage lanterns—reproductions of old-fashioned coach lights, designed for wall mounting;

hanging lanterns—similar in style to carriage lanterns, but designed to be hung from the ceiling;

globe lights—modern versions of the old carriage lantern, with a clear or opaque globe surrounding the bulb;

bulkhead light—functional ship-style light with a flush base and toughened glass or plastic cover, often with a wire grille for extra protection;

Left: A porch light illuminates the way to your front door, providing a warm welcome for guests, and also helps to deter unwelcome prowlers

brick light—similar to a bulkhead light, but with a plain rectangular or circular diffuser;

spotlight—special exterior types fitted with PAR (parabolic aluminised reflector) bulbs.

Whichever type you choose, it is vital that the lamp is designed for exterior use and is marked as such. Check carefully before you buy.

Planning the wiring

The wiring for the new light circuit must be run in 1.0mm² two-core and earth cable, and if it will be exposed on the outside wall of the house instead of running straight through the wall into the back of the fitting, it must be protected by high-impact plastic conduit sealed at the ends. Cable of this size must be protected by a 5-amp circuit fuse, so if you borrow power from a ring circuit you must do so via a fused connection unit containing a 5-amp fuse to provide the necessary sub-circuit protection (see Finding a power source).

In most cases, the best position for a porch light switch is just inside the hall door. However, a switch outside the house is also useful, allowing you to switch the light on when you come home and to find your front door key easily. If you use an outside switch, it must be a splashproof type. You can, of course, have both indoor and outdoor switches, wired up like those controlling your hall and landing lights indoors.

Finding a power source

The first job is to find an existing circuit into which you can tap to provide power for the new light (note that you can do this only for a light on the outside of the house wall; a remote light or lights must have its own independent circuit running from the consumer unit). You can tap into either a light circuit or a power circuit (as the illustrations overleaf explain), and the best place to look for a convenient connection point is usually underneath the upstairs floorboards, close to the projected position of the outside light.

The simplest way of making the connection is by inserting a four-terminal junction box into the existing lighting circuit cable (fig. A), and then

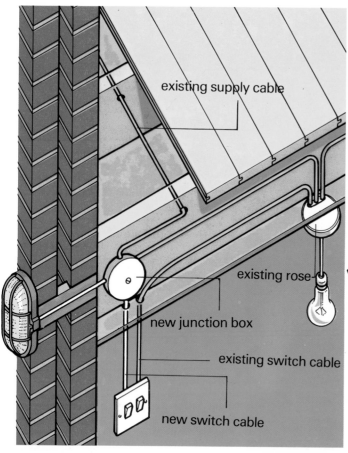

existing supply cable

existing rose

new junction box

existing switch cable

new switch cable

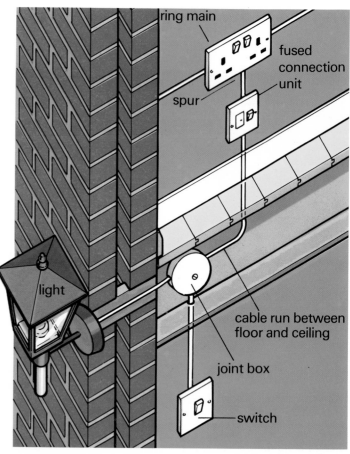

ring main

fused connection unit

spur

light

cable run between floor and ceiling

joint box

switch

running new cables on to the light and its switch. If there is no convenient circuit cable, you can run a spur cable from a three-terminal junction box cut into the nearest cable (see fig. E top) and then run new cable on to a four-terminal box from which the new light and switch cables will run (see fig. E bottom). If you have loop-in roses with banks of terminals, you may be able to run a spur cable from a nearby rose (fig. D) to a new four-terminal junction box, and then complete the wiring as shown in fig. E.

You can also take power from a ring circuit if this is more convenient. You can do this in one of three ways:
● by connecting a spur cable into the back of an existing socket outlet, so long as a spur is not already connected to it; the spur terminates in fused connection unit fitted with a 5-amp fuse (see fig. B)
● by connecting a spur cable to a 30-amp three-terminal junction box cut into the ring circuit at a convenient point; again a fused connection unit is used
● by connecting the fused connection unit directly into the ring circuit.

With these methods, 2.5mm² cable must be used for the spur to the fused connection unit; 1.0mm² cable is still used for the rest of the circuit.

Wiring to the new switch can be set in a chase cut in the plaster (fig. 2) or in

A. *One of the simplest ways of providing power for your new light is to insert a four-terminal junction box into an existing lighting circuit, and to run new cables on from this to the new light and switch*

B. *An alternative which may prove more convenient is to connect a spur to an upstairs socket outlet. This terminates in a fused connection unit fitted with a 5-amp fuse. The rest of the circuit is the same as in A*

1 *Once you have planned the cable routes, either cut chases in the plaster so you can conceal the cables or use surface-mounted mini-trunking*

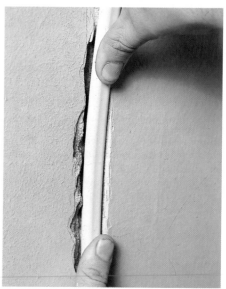

2 *Make sure the chases are deep enough for the cable to be buried completely and covered with plaster about 12mm (½in) thick*

3 *Run the cable through a hole in the wall immediately behind the light position, then mark the fixing holes on the wall surface*

4 *Mount the lamp baseplate on the wall. Then prepare the cable cores and connect them to the correct terminals on the light fitting*

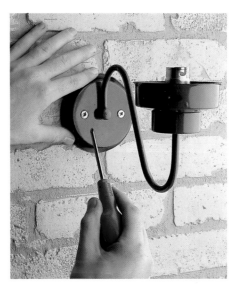

5 *Fold the cable and flex neatly into the mounting box and fit the lamp over it. Seal the box/wall junction with silicone mastic*

surface-mounted mini-trunking. It may be possible to utilise the cable drop to the existing hall light, and to replace this one-gang switch with a new two-gang one which would then control both porch and hall lights (fig. G).

Choose whichever wiring method is the most convenient in terms of short cable runs and accessibility.

Running the wiring

Once you have worked out where you will be taking the power from and where the new light and switch will be sited, you can start running in the new cables. It's best to run the cable for the light

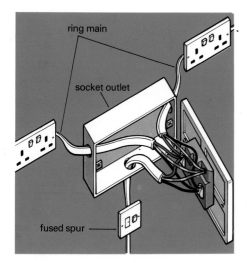

C. *Connect a spur cable into the terminals of an existing ring circuit socket as shown here, then run 2.5mm² cable on to the fused connection unit*

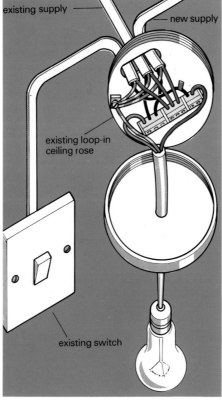

D: Above. *If you have loop-in wiring, you may be able to take a spur from an existing loop-in rose. Run it to a four-terminal box as shown in E*

E: Right. *Alternatively, take a spur from the existing circuit via a three-terminal box (top). In either case, the spur then runs to a four-terminal box and on to the light and switch*

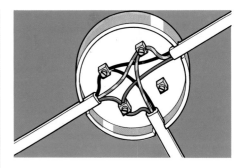

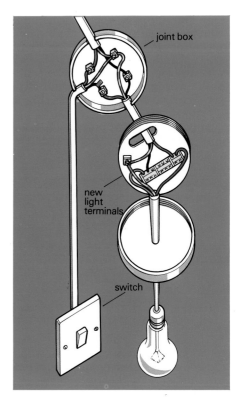

6 *If you are running your spur from a lighting or power circuit cable, isolate it and connect in a three-terminal junction box*

7 *Where cable runs have to cross joists, drill 12mm diameter holes through the joist centres. Secure runs parallel to joists with cable clips*

8 *If you are using the existing switch drop to the hall light position, replace the old one-gang switch with a two-gang type*

through the wall directly behind the fitting baseplate, so it's completely concealed from the outside. Drill a 10mm (⅜in) diameter hole through the wall at this point, sloping it slightly upwards so that any rainwater getting behind the baseplate cannot run through to the interior, and then thread a length of cable through. Leave a generous amount for connection to the light fitting.

Indoors, either cut chases so you can recess the cable into the wall surface (figs. 1 and 2), or else surface-mount it in mini-trunking. Complete the wiring, according to the method you have selected, right back to the point where it will be connected into the existing house wiring, but don't connect it up yet. Wire up the switch—one-gang or two-gang, according to your system requirements—as shown in figs. F, G and H.

Fixing the light
With most outside lights, you connect the cable cores directly to a small terminal block on or within the baseplate. The terminals may be marked L, N and E, or you may see short flex tails (colour-coded brown for live, blue for neutral and green/yellow for earth) running to a plastic terminal strip. If there is no earth terminal, check that the fitting is marked as being double-insulated.

With the cable connected up, attach the light baseplate to the wall with screws and wallplugs, and run a bead of clear silicone mastic round the base-

plate/wall junction to keep rainwater from penetrating it.

Connecting up the power
The final step is to connect up your new sub-circuit to the rest of the house wiring. Start by turning off the power at the main fusebox or consumer unit and then remove the fuse from the circuit concerned (if you have miniature circuit breakers, simply turn off the appropriate mcb). Check that the circuit is indeed dead by plugging in an appliance or turning on a light. Then make your final connections to the rose, socket or circuit cable as required.

If you are at all uncertain about making these final connections (or any part of the job), play safe and call in a qualified electrician.

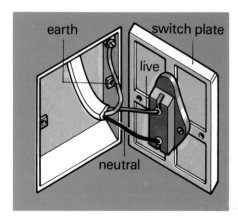

F. *If you are using a one-gang switch to control your new light, connect the red and black cores as shown and run the earth core to the box terminal*

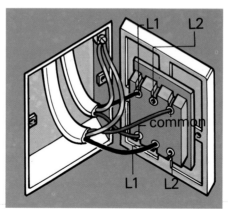

G. *If you are running the new light's switch cable down to the hall light position, fit a two-gang switch wired up as shown*

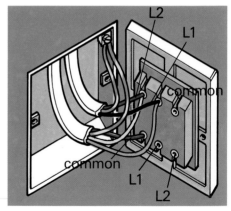

H. *If you are installing an outside switch too, link it to the indoor switch with three-core and earth cable to provide two-way switching*

INDEX

Picture credits

Advertising Arts 81(b); Kuo Kang Chen 120(t), 121(b), 122(b); Gavin Cochrane 16, 43, 49, 51, 52, 53(bc, br), 54, 84, 85, 114(b), 115(t), 116(t); Ray Duns 17, 22, 61, 67, 73, 74, 75(c, b), 95, 107; Bernard Fallon 69(tr, cr), 71, 76, 81(tl), 86, 89(b), 92, 94(b), 96; Nelson Hargreaves 40, 41; John Harwood/Trevor Lawrence 28; Hayward Art Group 44, 65, 66, 78(c, b), 81(tc); Dave King 119, 120(b), 121(t), 122(t); Trevor Lawrence 29; Nigel Messett 30, 39; Nick Mynheer 50; Colin Salmon 53(t); Terry Allen Designs 13; The Velux Co. Ltd. 87, 88, 89(t, c), 90, 91; Venner Artists 18(b), 20, 24, 37(t), 93(r), 105, 106, 108(t), 110(l), 111(tr), 112, 114(t), 116(c), 118; Gary Warren 14, 15(tl).